St Mark's Gospel
A COMMENTARY

NORMAN PRICE

RELIGIOUS AND MORAL EDUCATION PRESS
An Imprint of Arnold-Wheaton

Religious and Moral Education Press
An Imprint of Arnold-Wheaton
Hennock Road, Exeter EX2 8RP

Pergamon Press Ltd
Headington Hill Hall, Oxford OX3 0BW

Pergamon Press Inc.
Maxwell House, Fairview Park, Elmsford, New York 10523

Pergamon Press Canada Ltd
Suite 104, 150 Consumers Road, Willowdale, Ontario M2J 1P9

Pergamon Press (Australia) Pty Ltd
P.O. Box 544, Potts Point, N.S.W. 2011

Pergamon Press GmbH
Hammerweg 6, D-6242 Kronberg, Federal Republic of Germany

Copyright ©1983 Norman Price

All rights reserved. No part of this publication may be reproduced, stored in a retrieval system, or transmitted, in any form or by any means, electronic, electrostatic, magnetic tape, mechanical, photocopying, recording or otherwise, without permission in writing from the publishers.

First published 1983
Reprinted 1984

Printed in Great Britain by A. Wheaton & Co. Ltd, Exeter

ISBN 0 08-029250-X non net
ISBN 0 08-029251-8 net

Contents

Introduction	v
Mark, the Author	1
The Text	
Chapters 1–10: The Ministry of Jesus	5
Chapters 11–15: The Last Week	41
Appendix	64

Acknowledgements

The author and publisher wish to thank the following for permission to reproduce photographs in this book.

The Bridgeman Art Library (Albright Knox Collection, Buffalo, U.S.A.): p. 23
Middle East Photographic Archive: pp. 9, 16
Ronald Sheridan's Photo-Library: pp. 22, 40, 45, 47, 54, 61

The cover photograph is taken from the Book of Cerne and is reproduced by permission of the Syndics of Cambridge University Library.

Introduction

New ideas and information are continually coming to light in the study of the Christian religion. If the subject is to stay alive and healthy, these developments need to be explored and analysed, especially when they concern Biblical material and its interpretation. It has always been my belief and experience that out of sensible and open-minded study of such material many other issues and considerations – moral, social, ethical and even political – could and should arise. If the Bible is to be seen as relevant today, then it must undergo the same scrutiny with regard to its value and truths as do other areas of study.

With this in mind, I have produced some 'Class-room Commentaries' on the gospels. I have chosen that title because my notes are a gathering together of ideas, research and discussions over many years of preparing candidates for examinations in Religious Studies, but of course the 'class-room' extends to all would-be students of the gospels, of all ages, denominations and backgrounds.

We begin with Mark, because that was the first gospel to appear. It soon becomes obvious that if we possessed only this one gospel our knowledge and understanding of the life and teaching of Jesus would be more restricted. In Mark's record we find that much of the familiar 'Life of Christ' material is missing. However, on studying other gospels we shall see how those writers supplement his account with material from their own sources. In this way, the 'synoptic' question is put more clearly into focus.

Teachers and students alike will know that examiners are increasingly looking for evidence from candidates of up-to-date background information, together with the candidates' own assessment and evaluation of incidents and ideas. I have therefore incorporated these requirements into the notes. I have not included a text of the gospel (though chapter and verse references are given throughout) because I have always found it a very useful exercise to consult as many different translations as possible, provided that they are read in conjunction with the notes.

I have worked within a definite framework of requirements for G.C.E. O level and similar examinations and it is obvious that, in this kind of commentary, every aspect and incident cannot be dealt with at great length. However, there are plenty of suggestions and ideas which can be explored and developed by the student as time and opportunity allow.

Norman Price
Head of Religious Studies
Torquay Grammar School

Palestine

Mark, the Author

The Christian 'gospel' was not primarily a book at all. The word, from the Anglo-Saxon 'god-spel', meant 'God narrative', but originally it was a reward paid to someone bearing good news and then came to be used for the message itself. So the gospel was the good news about God brought by Jesus, preached by the Apostles and written down by the gospel writers. The writers are sometimes called the Evangelists, from the Latin 'evangelium', which in turn is based on the Greek word 'evangelion', meaning 'to bring good news'. One examination candidate once called them 'Accountants' because his teacher had often talked of the 'accounts' given by these writers. One thing is certain: the gospels are not biographies of Jesus and were never intended to be. They are quick word pictures, not detailed portraits where the subject sat patiently to be painted and not photographs catching every detail. There was obviously very much more of the life and teaching of Jesus than has been recorded in the four gospels.

Who was Mark?

A bishop named Papias who lived in Asia Minor about A.D. 130 wrote that he himself had been told that 'Mark, having been the interpreter of Peter, wrote accurately, though not in order, all that he had recalled of what had been said and done by the Lord'. Also Irenaeus, when Bishop of Lyons about A.D. 180, wrote 'after the deaths of Peter and Paul, Mark, the disciple and interpreter of Peter, handed down to us in writing the things Peter had proclaimed'.

If this is the John Mark mentioned in the Acts of the Apostles as the cousin of Barnabas, as well as in several of Paul's letters, and in a letter by Peter, then we know his mother was named Mary and that she had a house in Jerusalem where the early Christians used to meet (Acts 12: 12). It may well have been the house where the Last Supper was held. Some say that Mark was the 'young man' who tried to warn Jesus on the night of Jesus's arrest (Mark 14: 51), but there is little evidence for that.

Where did Mark get his information?

Some of it probably came from Peter, although the belief that he got it all from Peter is not now widely held. He may well have had some information from the Christians who met at his home and there were obviously written sources of material on which he could draw, especially on the events of the Last Supper, trials and death of Jesus. Some of these written sources are referred to by Luke in the preface to his gospel (1: 1).

When did Mark's gospel appear?
About A.D. 65.

Why was it so long after the life of Jesus before such a record was produced?
There are various reasons. For example:

1. Jesus died when he was only a young man, so for years there were plenty of people around who had been eyewitnesses to the events and who would tell the stories themselves.
2. Many people believed that Jesus would soon return to the earth (the second coming) and it would be the end of the age. Also, presumably, Jesus could repeat his teaching if necessary.
3. Many people could not read or write, but they were expert in remembering things accurately, so an oral method of teaching was preferred.

Why was it written down?
Main reasons:

1. Because eyewitnesses were dying off and personal contact was being lost.
2. The Church was spreading and missionaries needed accurate records.
3. False teachers were spreading a corrupted version of the stories, so authentic accounts were needed.
4. After the burning of Rome in A.D. 64 Nero, the Emperor, blamed the Christians for the fire to avert suspicion from himself, and a terrible persecution of the Christians began. Many died, including Peter and Paul, but before he died, Peter persuaded Mark to write down some of the important events in the life of Jesus. Mark probably used his account of these events to supplement certain written records, especially of the last few days in the life of Jesus, which he already had. So probably his gospel was written 'backwards', with the ending being put down first.

The main aims of Mark's gospel

1. To try to answer certain questions which exercised the minds of the early Christians. For example, how and why did Jesus die, and who was responsible for his death? What was his attitude towards the Sabbath and towards the leaders of the Jewish religion? What did it mean to be a true disciple?
2. To bring comfort to persecuted Christians. Mark was writing in a time of great crisis and to people in great need. That is why he included so many miracle stories, rather than parables. He concentrated on what Jesus did rather than what he said, because he wanted to show how Jesus could help people in trouble.

3. To show that those who witness for Christ do so as evidence of what they know to be true. It may well mean martyrdom for them.

His style of writing

The gospels were all written in Greek. At the beginning of the first century A.D. there were more Jews living outside Palestine than within it and Greek was the most widely used language. Mark's Greek was not very polished or very educated. It was the everyday Greek of the ordinary person with one or two Aramaic words put in and translated for his non-Jewish readers: words such as 'Boanerges' (sons of thunder) (3: 17), 'Talitha cumi' (Get up, my child) (5: 41) and 'Ephphatha' (Be opened) (7: 34). Aramaic was the local language Jesus would have spoken. Mark gives the impression of being always in a hurry to get on with the story and his favourite word is 'immediately' (Revised Standard Version) or 'straightway' (Authorized Version). The word occurs over forty times.

The synoptic gospels

Most scholars are agreed that Mark's gospel record was the first to appear (almost certainly written in Rome in about A.D. 65), followed by Luke and Matthew in the space of about fifteen years. When we see how Luke and Matthew copied and used Mark we realize that such a thing as copyright did not exist! Of Mark's 676 verses Luke uses about 350 and Matthew about 600, sometimes changing or adding to the details, so that their plan and pattern are very similar. Thus we give these first three gospels the name 'syn-optic', meaning 'same view' or 'seen together'. John's gospel is very different from the other three.

If Mark's gospel was the first to be written, why is Matthew's first in the New Testament order of the gospels?

It is probably because in the early Church Matthew became their teaching gospel since he seemed to answer many of their questions and included much of the teaching of Jesus, especially the Sermon on the Mount. But we must remember that the order, or canon, of the New Testament books was not decided finally until some time in the fourth century A.D.

Why don't all the gospels tell the same stories?

When one gospel is compared with another it becomes obvious that there are differences, even apparent contradictions. Each writer has his own aims and purposes in presenting his account and each adds to the picture of Jesus – something like a photo-fit picture built up from different descriptions. Like spotlights from four different corners of a theatre, they all shine on the same figures on the stage but they are sometimes different colours and sometimes pick out different details of the drama. It is these variations which, to me at least, underline their honesty. If they were all word for word the same, I would suspect their reliability. But certainly, if we had only one of the gospel records instead of four, our understanding of the life and teaching of Jesus would be much more restricted. It is interesting, after looking at them all, to try to decide which, if we had to choose, would be the one selected for survival.

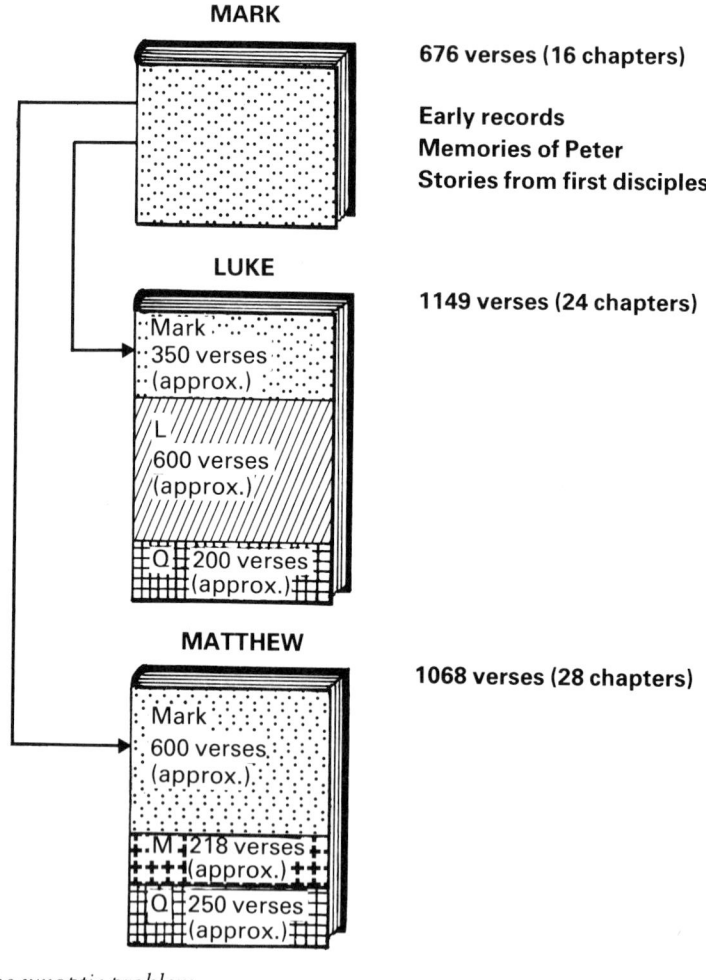

The synoptic problem

The Text
Chapters 1-10: The Ministry of Jesus

CHAPTER 1

vv. 1–3 Title and Introduction

Some translators have 'the gospel *of* Jesus Christ', others say '*about* Jesus'. It was the good news that he brought, taught and showed by the way he lived. The name 'Jesus' is the Greek form of the Old Testament name Joshua. 'Christ' is not a name but a title. The Hebrew word 'Messiah' means 'anointed one' and the Greek work 'Christos' and the English word 'Christ' mean the same. He was not *a* Son of God, which was sometimes used in the Old Testament for a good man, but *the* Son of God. Mark is a bit mixed up about the prophecies: v. 2 is from Malachi 3: 1, v. 3 is from Isaiah 40: 3.

vv. 4–8 John the Baptizer

John saw himself as fulfilling the prophecies of Malachi and Isaiah, i.e. preparing the way for the coming Messiah, but dressing and preaching like his great Old Testament hero, the prophet Elijah. Elijah was the original prophet of what we sometimes call social justice: for example, in the incident of Naboth's vineyard, he condemned the greed and injustice of Ahab and Jezebel and their terrible ill-treatment of Naboth (1 Kings 21). In Luke 3 we can see how John emphasizes this side of religion. John's food was the fare of poor people; the locusts may well have been the beans of the locust or carob tree. Baptism was the public sign of private repentance – the washing away of sins and making a fresh start. John's relation to Jesus was that of a servant and a slave. He said he was not worthy even to stoop down and untie his sandals. John's baptism was with water, Jesus's baptism would be the cleansing of sin by the power of God's Holy Spirit.

vv. 9–11 The baptism of Jesus

Mark does not say anything about the birth or boyhood of Jesus. Jesus suddenly appeared on the scene and was baptized by John in the River Jordan, probably at a place known as Bethabara.

QUESTIONS

Why, in Mark, are there no birth stories about Jesus?
  There are various possibilities:

1. He did not know them.
2. He knew them but did not believe them.
3. He did not think his readers would believe them.

4. He did not think they were a vital part of the gospel record, and he had to choose his material very carefully.
5. He thought they might detract from the picture of the 'human' Jesus he was trying to portray.

The birth stories of Jesus, and of John the Baptist, are to be found in Luke and Matthew.

If baptism was for repentance and washing away of sins, why was Jesus baptized?
   It may have been:
1. to identify himself with John's work and to show support for John.
2. to show he was one of the people, not aloof from them.
3. to share the needs of his fellow men.

Was this the moment when Jesus became conscious of his 'call' to serve God, as had happened to many of the Old Testament prophets, or had he been aware of all this ever since he was a boy of twelve (Luke 2: 49)? There is no easy answer but plenty of scope for suggestions. Part of the difficulty is that we know little or nothing about his life from the age of twelve to his late twenties, when he was baptized. This is the first occasion on which the 'voice from heaven' is heard. There are two other times: Mark 9: 7 and John 12: 28. The words are a quotation from Isaiah 42: 1, from what is known as one of the 'suffering servant' poems. This shows what kind of Messiah Jesus intended to be.

vv. 12–13   The temptations

Mark gives no details of these. We have to go to Luke 4 and Matthew 4 for a fuller account. They were using a written document which Mark did not possess; it is called 'Q' from the German word 'Quelle', meaning 'source' or 'spring'.

Obviously Jesus had to have time and quiet to think things over after his baptism. What did being 'God's Beloved Son' mean? What was he going to do with the powers he now possessed? What kind of Messiah was he going to be? How would he attract people to God? All these questions are discussed in the studies of the accounts of the temptations in the other gospels.

vv. 14–15   Jesus begins his work

Mark's prologue and introduction, the first thirteen verses, are over. Now the story can begin. John the Baptist had been put in prison. (Mark gives the explanation for this in Ch. 6.) Just how much did the work of John and Jesus overlap? According to Mark not very much, if at all, but John's gospel tells us of some overlapping (3: 22–36). In Mark's gospel, from this point until 7: 24, Jesus is in and around Galilee. Like John the Baptist, he begins by telling people to 'repent' because the Kingdom of God is at hand. (*Note*   Mark calls it 'the Kingdom of God'; Matthew (4: 17, for example) calls it 'the Kingdom of Heaven'.)

What did Jesus mean by 'the Kingdom'? Not a geographical place ruled over by an earthly king. Not a division of people based on language, or colour, or race, but a way of life, beliefs about God, and standards of behaviour. These things were a condition of entry into 'the Kingdom'. In Matthew's gospel many of the parables are about 'the Kingdom' because one of the writer's main aims is to show Jesus as the 'King', spiritually, and 'the Kingdom' he would set up in the hearts and lives of people.

vv. 16–20   Jesus's recruits

Jesus needed friends and help in his work. Thus his next step was to choose companions and followers. 'Disciple' originally meant learner or student. From it we get the word 'discipline'. A good student or disciple has to have self-discipline.

The first four to be chosen were fishermen, two pairs of brothers – Simon, Andrew, James and John.

Why choose fishermen? What was so special about *these* men? What qualities did they possess?

 Patience – they often fished all night, sometimes for nothing.
 Courage – the Sea of Galilee was a dangerous place.
 Common sense – practical, no-nonsense men.
 Hard-working, conscientious men.

Jesus did not choose them because they were particularly religious or good. He saw their potential, like a sculptor seeing the possibilities of a piece of wood or stone. He did not say to these men, 'When you are better I will come back for you', or 'When you have passed all your exams I will take you on', or 'When I see you in the synagogue every Saturday I will consider you'. He took them as they were and he would make them into what he wanted them to be – 'fishers of men'.

Had they ever met Jesus before?   Yes, I would think they had and would have talked to him often about this kind of adventure. I don't think they just threw down their oars and went off with a complete stranger, leaving their father or brothers or hired men to do all the work. Men as selfish as that would not have made very good disciples.

Were they married and did they have any families?   Not much is known about that but Peter, at least, was married, for Jesus healed his mother-in-law (1: 31).

vv. 21–34   A day in the life of Jesus

It is a rare thing in the gospels to follow Jesus through a whole day. It was the Sabbath (Saturday), the seventh day of the week. The Jews took the Genesis story of creation literally. God had created the world and everything in it in six days, then rested on the seventh day. Their word for 'rest' was 'shabbath', so it was a day of rest. It lasted from sunset on Friday, when a call of the trumpet would tell everyone it was time to stop work, whatever they were doing, until sunset on the Saturday. Christians keep Sunday, the first day of the week, as their Holy Day because it was the day of the resurrection.

The place was Capernaum, at the northern end of Lake Galilee. It was a busy port on the road to Damascus and was probably where Matthew had his toll-booth to collect taxes.

The synagogue (from the Greek word meaning 'bringing together') was the local Jewish place of worship and there was one in every village. There was only one temple and that was in Jerusalem. Jesus went to the synagogue every Sabbath (Luke 4: 16). The service consisted of readings from the Law of Moses and the Prophets, together with the singing of psalms and the saying of prayers. The ruler or president of the synagogue (Jairus was one of these – 5: 22) could invite any distinguished visitor to speak. The question arises: was Jesus a qualified teacher or preacher? Perhaps not in the usual sense, but the disciples often called him 'Rabbi', which meant 'teacher' or 'master'. What *was* sure is that his sermon made them sit up and take notice.

The scribes were men who were not only copyists of the law but also interpreters of difficult passages. They copied the law mainly for teaching purposes, though they would also provide copies for individuals to study, since copying by hand was the only way of reproducing the law. At one time, in the Old Testament, a scribe was just a writer who was employed to write on a scroll at someone else's dictation, but in Jesus's day it was a much more elevated office and a scribe enjoyed considerable power and influence and might sometimes be called a 'lawyer'. Some had their own schools and taught their own interpretations of the law, while others toured the country and led discussions at synagogues. They were fond of argument and debate, as we shall see in the gospels. Often their sermons were dull and boring, merely repeating what the scribes had read in books, but on that Saturday morning it was different. The people said that Jesus spoke 'with authority', meaning personal knowledge and experience of God. The congregation liked his preaching *and* his personality.

The interruption It was believed in those days that disease, especially mental illness, was due to a person being possessed by demons. The sick man evidently believed this because he speaks of 'us' (v. 24). He also recognizes the miraculous powers of Jesus. Jesus exorcized (drove out) the evil spirits from the man. The question arises: did Jesus believe in exorcism or was he just healing in the only way such people could understand? Everybody was amazed at this event and went home to tell other people.

v. 29   Next came lunch at Peter's house. But first Jesus cured the fever of Peter's

The Upper Galilee plain

mother-in-law, who obviously lived with them. Then at sunset, when the Sabbath was over and 'work' could begin again, they carried sick people to him and Jesus worked far into the night healing them. What a day it had been – what a picture of Jesus! A bit different from the usual picture some people have of him, which I often call 'the stained-glass-window' Jesus.

v. 35 Then next morning he was up at the crack of dawn and out to a lonely place to pray and get strength for the day.

If Jesus was so busy when did he compose his excellent parables and prepare his preaching? They were not 'off the cuff' efforts! It was probably at just such a time as this, in the early morning, when he was alone and quiet.

vv. 37–38 Mark often talks of the crowds who were seeking Jesus; this shows how popular he was. Peter's remark sounds almost like a reprimand of Jesus, which would be rather typical of impulsive Peter, as we shall see on other occasions, e.g. his 'confession' (8: 32). If Peter *was* rebuking Jesus for not staying in Capernaum, Jesus soon showed that he was not going to be persuaded or pressurized into going back there. He told the disciples that he wanted to go on to other places to preach – possibly implying to Peter that *his* home town was no more important than anyone else's!

v. 39 This shows how much is missing from our knowledge of Jesus's preaching.

vv. 40–45 The leper

Leprosy was a loathsome disease and common in those days, although the word was sometimes used to denote various skin diseases. A leper was considered unclean in body *and* spirit because it was assumed that a terrible sin had been committed to cause the disease. According to the law of Moses, to touch a leper made the toucher unclean but Jesus did not mind that. What he *did* seem to mind was the man's attitude because v. 41 literally means 'being angry with him' and v. 43 ('thrust him out with this stern warning') also indicates anger.

Why should Jesus be angry with the man?

1. For approaching him? It was not like Jesus to mind that.
2. For doubting Jesus's willingness or ability to heal him?
3. Because he was not a very honest character?
4. Or was Jesus angry at the conditions of the time?

Whatever the reason the man proved to be untrustworthy. He could not even do the one thing Jesus asked him, which was to keep quiet. But could one really expect him to?

CHAPTER 2 THE BEGINNING OF OPPOSITION TO JESUS

How odd that after expecting the Messiah for seven hundred years, now that he had come, the very people who had looked forward to his coming turned against him. If an evangelist or missionary came to your area, wouldn't you expect the local churches to help him? Would you expect your church leaders to make plans to discredit him? And if they did, and you met him and liked him a lot better than your own church leaders, what then?

Why did the Pharisees begin to turn against Jesus, and so soon, according to Mark?

The word 'Pharisee' meant 'separated one'. This idea of separateness can often be a dangerous one: exclusive usually implies 'superior' and certainly some of the Pharisees thought they were God's chosen men. They were also expecting a *Jewish* Messiah who would obey all the Jewish rules and regulations, which Jesus apparently did not, as we shall see.

In this chapter Mark gives us three examples of why the Jewish religious leaders began to turn against Jesus.

vv. 1–12 Blasphemy

The four men who brought their friend to Jesus to be healed showed a great deal of faith and determination. When they could not get in through the door they broke through the roof, although one hopes that they offered to pay for the damage!

Whose house was it? Verse 1 says he was 'at home', but Jesus's home was in

Nazareth. It sounds as though it was the home of the one who was telling the story, which was Peter. It could not have been Mark's house since we know he lived in Jerusalem. Some commentators, thinking of the difficulties involved in getting the man up on to the roof (though this would not necessarily be difficult as many houses had outside stairs leading up to the flat roof), then down on ropes into the room, suggest that Mark was exaggerating the incident a little. But surely the whole point of emphasizing the effort involved was to show what faith the friends had, which Jesus warmly commends.

Part of the cure was to convince the man that his sins were forgiven: that his illness was not the cause or the result of sin. However, the Pharisees took strong exception to Jesus pronouncing a forgiveness of sins. They believed that only God could do that: for a *man* to claim to do it was seen as blasphemy.

The term 'Son of Man', which Jesus uses here, had a long history. In the Book of Daniel it meant a human being but in two later Jewish books, written about 100 B.C., it meant a supernatural Messiah. In the Book of Ezekiel the expression is used ninety-four times, but always meaning 'a man'. Here, Jesus was perhaps using the word in both senses.

vv. 13–17   Associating with sinners (Dining with the 'outcasts')

A tax-collector was an outcast as far as the Jews were concerned, not merely because he was often a cheat and a profiteer but mainly because he worked for the hated Roman authorities. The Romans would sell a tax district by auction and the man who bought it had to provide a set amount of money from that area in taxation. As long as he handed over that sum he could pocket any extra he made by overcharging or cheating. The Jews did not mind paying their temple taxes – their religious dues – but they resented paying what they regarded as pagan taxes, and they hated the men who collected them. The Roman word for their own tax-collectors was 'publicani', so the Jewish collectors were sometimes called 'publicans'.

Jesus not only invited Levi (called 'Matthew' by Luke and Matthew) to be a disciple, which was bad enough, but he also accepted an invitation to a dinner given by Levi, presumably to say farewell to his friends. One wonders what the other tax-collectors thought of him giving up a well-paid comfortable job to go off with a travelling preacher! To the Jews, to eat with someone was a sign of friendship and sympathy, so they were disgusted at Jesus associating with such people.

Jesus's quotation about the doctor was very apt. You have to admit that you are ill before you seek the help of a doctor and the doctor cannot do much for you if you do not bother to consult him. The Pharisees would not admit to being in need of any help or forgiveness.

vv. 23–28   Breaking the Sabbath rules ('Crime' in the cornfield)

The Jewish Sabbath was like a tailor's shop window today: all the models frozen in one position, looking like people but with no life in them. People were almost afraid to breathe, and virtually any movement could be seen as 'work'. For example, a chair dragged through the earthen floor might be 'ploughing', a needle carried in a coat could be 'sewing' and, although feeding of hens was allowed, the feeder had to take care that none of the corn became covered up for that would be 'sowing'. Followers of certain Jewish rabbis even argued that to eat an egg which had been laid on the Sabbath was wrong because the hen had 'worked' in laying it! These were extremes, of course, but there are always people who love going to extremes in order to be sensational. So when the disciples picked ears of corn, rubbed off the husks in their hands and ate the corn, they were apparently 'reaping and threshing' on the Sabbath day. In fact Jesus himself was not accused, only the disciples were, but he defended them. For Jesus to say (v. 28) that he was 'Lord and Master over the Sabbath' and not bound by its rules would horrify the Pharisees even more. What he was really saying was that human need is more important than the Sabbath laws.

The odd thing about v. 26 is that Mark has got the name of the High Priest wrong. If you check the story in 1 Samuel 21, you will see that the High Priest was really Ahimelech, not Abiathar. When Matthew comes to copy the story (Matthew 12: 1–7) he, an expert on the Old Testament, realizes that Mark has got it wrong, but instead of correcting it he cleverly omits to name the Priest at all!

CHAPTER 3

vv. 1–6 A 'put-up' job

Up to this point his critics had only grumbled at Jesus, or the disciples, but now they were actually plotting to kill him. Why? Not only for healing on the Sabbath, but for putting his critics to shame. To be shown up and bettered by someone you dislike is always hard to bear.

This case of the man with the crippled arm seems to be a put-up job. He had probably been placed in the front row and perhaps paid to take part. St Luke (6: 6) says it was his right arm that was crippled and Jerome, who gave us the Latin translation of the Bible, the Vulgate, says that the man was a stone-mason. The law allowed only very urgent cases to be treated on the Sabbath and this man was not seriously ill. He had been put there by the Pharisees to see what Jesus would do. Jesus not only healed him, but made *them* look foolish. He asked whether they wanted him to do good or evil. Refusal to do good is often an encouragement to evil. They could hardly have said 'evil', so they remained silent, but seething. Jesus was angry (v. 5) at their stupidity and short-sightedness.

It is a good exercise, sometimes, to write down what we mean by doing good on our holy day and also the things that make us angry.

The Herodians (v. 6) are mentioned only in Mark. They were evidently supporters of Herod Antipas, tetrarch or ruler over Galilee, son of the Herod who killed the babies when Jesus was born.

vv. 7–12 The crowds

A feature of Mark's gospel is the frequent mention of the crowds of people that followed Jesus wherever he went. This was referred to earlier in 1: 37. This time the crowd was so great that Jesus had to preach from a boat, perhaps Peter's, to avoid being crushed. Later on (6: 31) Mark says that Jesus was so hemmed in and harassed by the crowd that he had no time 'even to eat'. That is a bit different from the usual picture of Jesus. This is the *real* Jesus – no rest and no respite from demands made upon him all the time.

vv. 13–19 The Twelve

Why twelve? Because there were twelves tribes in the old Israel and these twelve were to be Jesus's representatives in the new Israel. It may also have been the idea of the remnant (or a few) being the nucleus of the new order, as put forward by Isaiah 10: 20–21. It was the intensive training of the few from whom great things could come. The same idea is expressed in certain parables, e.g. Mark 4: 30.

Note that he called those 'whom he wanted' (v. 13). There were probably many applicants and Jesus selected just the ones he needed. But what a strange selection they were and how odd that we hear a lot about some of them (Peter, James and John), a little about others (Andrew, Philip, Thomas and Judas) and nothing at all about the rest, unless Bartholomew is another name for Nathaniel (John 1: 45). Why choose them and not use them, or do we have records of only the incidents where the main characters were involved?

Why did Jesus give some of them nicknames? Probably because a name implied a person's character or at least what he hoped to be. Peter (Greek 'Petros', Aramaic 'Cephas') meant 'rock' or 'stone'. On the shores of Lake Galilee today there is a little church built over the huge rock on which Jesus is supposed to have stood when he saw Peter fishing and decided to give him that nickname. Peter did not always live up to such a strong reputation.

'Boanerges', for James and John, may have meant that they had loud voices or fiery tempers or even that their father was a shouter. Some have suggested it was because they wanted to call down fire from heaven on the Samaritan village (Luke 9: 54). Simon the Zealot was a member of an underground movement in Galilee called the Zealots who were dedicated to the overthrow and defeat of the occupying Roman Army. They waged guerrilla warfare against the Romans for over sixty years, until A.D.66.

Judas, whose name came from the honoured Old Testament name of Judah, was, according to John 13: 2, the son of Simon Iscariot. But Iscariot could also have been a nickname from the Latin word 'sicarius' meaning 'assassin' and may have been applied to Judas later on. 'Sicarius' was also the Roman nickname for a Zealot, and some think that Judas might have belonged to that organization, but that is very unlikely since he was not a Galilean. Other suggestions are 'man of Kerioth' and 'from the tribe of Issachar'. He was the only one of the twelve who was not from Galilee and was certainly the odd one out. According to John 12: 6, he was also the keeper of the purse for the disciples' money.

How did Jesus get such a varied group to work together so well? Probably by his powerful personality and sense of purpose. It is often overlooked how remarkable it was that he persuaded, for example, Simon the Zealot to work with Matthew the tax-collector. It is a lesson in human relationships.

vv. 20–30   He's mad!

They didn't mean that Jesus was insane. It was like saying of someone who is doing far too much, or working far too hard, 'he must be out of his mind'. The scribes soon latched on to the idea and said that Jesus was also in league with the devil. In fact, they said, he had control over demons because he was directed by the prince of all demons 'Beelzebub', or 'Lord of the mansions'. To this Jesus replied, using the idea of a mansion, 'How can a house divided against itself stand up?' In other words, 'If I *were* in league with the devil wouldn't I want to make people worse, not better?' The devil's work is evil, not good.

So again his answer proved too clever for his critics, and to emphasize the point he said that sin against the Holy Spirit can never be forgiven (v. 29). This is a very difficult phrase, but it seems to mean that the sin for which there is no forgiveness is just what the Pharisees had been doing, i.e. calling good evil. It is a widespread practice today.

vv. 31–35   Jesus's family

There is no mention of Joseph. What had happened to him? Perhaps he had died as he was probably quite a bit older than Mary. Who were 'Jesus's brothers'? It depends of course on what is meant by brothers. Some Christians, wanting to safeguard the perpetual virginity of Mary, say the word means 'cousins', or 'friends', or even 'half-brothers' – children of Joseph by a former marriage. Others take the word as it stands, and in fact Mark 6: 3 actually names Jesus's brothers and mentions his sisters. Whatever the truth, Jesus says here that all who do God's will are his family, which would be a great comfort to Mark's readers in their time of persecution and broken relationships. Jesus was not being indifferent to family ties, he was just putting God's claim first.

CHAPTER 4   TEACHING BY PARABLES

In the western world we generally try to express our ideas in fairly plain language, but eastern people like to colour their ideas with images and illustrations. It is a kind of picture language, which, not surprisingly, is used a lot in the Bible since the Bible is an eastern book. From the Bible it can be seen that preachers and prophets very often used parables to illustrate the points they were trying to put over. An interesting idea on some of the parables in the gospels is that they were originally illustrations which Jesus had used in his synagogue sermons, and though the sermon had been forgotten – or perhaps used elsewhere in the gospel – the parable illustration had been remembered. This could be why so few of the parables are explained – they might well have been used originally to illustrate something else. Certainly, if you try out this idea on someone who went to church last Sunday, the chances are that they will have forgotten the sermon but remembered a story the preacher told in the sermon.

The word 'parable' comes from the Greek, meaning 'to put side by side', to compare, and many of the stories about the Kingdom begin 'The Kingdom of heaven is like. . . .' Some illustration from everyday experience was taken and used to show what the Kingdom is like or how to get into it, or how to behave in it, and since Jesus lived among people who made their living mainly from farming or fishing, many of his stories were taken from these kinds of background. Other parables could be called 'example stories' where people in certain situations, rather than sheep or seeds, were used to show how we should behave towards one another and to show God's attitude towards us. So a parable is much more than 'an earthly story with a heavenly meaning'.

Why are there so few parables in Mark? Possibly because he did not know them (nearly all of them are found in Luke or Matthew), but more likely because he was far more interested in the miracles of Jesus than in the parables. Also, he gives the impression of always being in a hurry, so he gives only a selection of parables because of pressure of time and space.

vv. 1–2   Again Mark mentions the crowds; this time they were all over the beach. The boat was probably Peter's.

vv. 3–9   The sower and the soil

In those days few people had any gardens to their houses. Instead they had plots of ground, like allotments, outside the village. There would be well-trodden footpaths between them and any stones would be dug up and put along the borders of the plot of land. Inevitably weeds would appear amongst them. A farmer's fields, which were often small, would be marked out in a similar way, not with hedges but with boundary stones – quite different from our fields. Sometimes a field would have a lot of stones in it, far too many to be cleared away, so the 'stony soil' and the 'good ground' would be mixed together. After the ploughman had prepared the ground with his light one-hand-operated plough, which sometimes did not make much of a mark, the sower would follow behind scattering the seed from a seed-bag or tray, and however skilled he was some seed would fall on soil trodden down hard by the turning oxen or where weeds were growing.

So this is not really a parable about the sower, but about the soil. It is the story of how people respond to the gospel challenge. Some are quite indifferent (the footpath people) or at least have lost any sense of need, some start off well then give up when the going gets hard (the stones), some start off with good intentions then other interests or ambitions crowd out religion in their lives and they forget about it (the thorns). Some, however, respond well (the good soil) but even then the response varies. The hundredfold people are exceptional servants of God – that is why we admire them so much. One wonders whether Jesus, as he told this parable, asked his listeners actually to rub out ears of corn and count the grains.

A point often raised about this parable is that since the good ground was only one of four places mentioned the success rate of the sowing was only 25 per cent, but quite obviously *most* of the seed would fall on the good ground. A more valid point is that all sowing involved risk and some loss, as every teacher knows. This parable is really the story of Jesus's own work: some of his preaching was successful, some was not.

vv. 10–12 Why did Jesus tell parables?

The simple answer would seem to be because many of his listeners could not read or write and a story based on a familiar, everyday event would appeal to their imaginations and would be remembered. But here, according to Mark, and the quotation from Isaiah 6: 9–10, it would appear that Jesus taught in parables in order to hide the truth, rather than reveal it. Possibly some of his hearers *did* find the parables a little difficult to understand, or perhaps they preferred to misunderstand them, but it is hard to imagine that Jesus was trying to confuse rather than clarify. Such an idea would be contrary to the point of this parable, which was all about people *responding* to the gospel. Verse 12 may possibly mean 'They see, but do not really understand', or perhaps, as some scholars suggest, these three verses are an insertion by someone who put in their own particular – and perverse – ideas on the parables.

Threshing with yoked oxen in Syria

vv. 13–20 Jesus explained the parable, which was unusual. Out of the forty or so parables, or fragments of parables, preserved in the gospels, there are records of Jesus explaining only two of them – this one of the Sower and the one about the Weeds in the Wheat (Matthew 13).

Why didn't he explain more of them? Perhaps he did and the writers did not record it (see v. 34). Then, isn't there a danger in everyone putting their own interpretations on the parables? Perhaps, but if we had the interpretation that might make us think there was only one explanation. If one considers a parable like the Prodigal Son (Luke 15: 11), for example, the lessons from it are endless. How could the writers give just one? Also we can never be sure that the explanation we have is the one that Jesus actually gave, for in this parable the emphasis is on the soil and in the explanation it is on the seed, which does not really fit the parable.

Fragments of parables

vv. 21–22 The lamp on the stand
Just as the purpose of a lamp is to give light, so must people of the light show it in their lives. The truth Jesus preached must one day be revealed.

vv. 24–25 The measure
This seems to mean that the one who gives generously when selling can expect good measure when buying. In other words, a person who shows mercy can expect mercy in return. It is a quality of life and one to be used, not neglected.

Parables of growth

vv. 26–29 The growing seed
The sole parable to be found only in Mark. The growth of the kingdom is silent and secret, yet secure. Man sows the seed, God provides the increase. It is the mystery of growth and the power of growth: it is gradual – by stages – but the harvest will one day come.

vv. 30–32 The mustard seed
A story of great things from small beginnings. In the sub-tropical climate of the Jordan river valley, the bush known as 'black mustard' grows wild and often reaches the height of a horse and rider, so it *is* the largest of all plants, as Mark says. This story is true not only of mighty rivers and trees but also of great movements and ideas. The Christian gospel began with one man and a few friends, now it is in every country and has been translated into many hundreds of languages. The 'birds' in v. 32 may mean the gentile peoples who will enter the Kingdom.

Miracles of Jesus (4: 35 – 5: 43)

This section, to the end of Chapter 5, deals with four miracles of Jesus which Mark uses to demonstrate Jesus's power over nature, mental illness, physical illness and death.

What are 'miracles'? Is the dictionary definition satisfactory? Is a miracle just a 'supernatural event'? Is it a force or event which cannot be explained by science? What is the difference between the miraculous events in the Old Testament, such as the crossing of the Reed Sea in the Exodus from Egypt (Reed Sea, not Red Sea, is the actual translation of the Hebrew words), or the crossing of the Jordan to capture Jericho, and the miracles of Jesus? Were not the Old Testament events sometimes a question of timing, which is often the sense in which we use the word 'miracle' today? Something happens at the right moment and we say 'it was a miracle' that such and such a thing occurred.

Consider the words of St Augustine, 'Miracles are not contrary to Nature but to what is known of Nature.'

In what ways did Jesus use what we now call mental therapy – a psychological approach before a physical cure could be made? We must remember that almost a third of Mark's gospel tells of miracles. These were events which had happened within the living memory of many of his readers. People who had witnessed them were amazed and sometimes disturbed, but never disbelieving. Even Jesus's enemies saw them as signs of his miraculous powers.

Why did Jesus perform miracles? Never to help himself or to please himself and never to force people to believe in him. They were done for a variety of reasons – out of pity, in response to faith or appeal, to help people in need, and so on.

How much does our belief in Jesus as the Messiah and the Son of God depend on these stories of his miraculous powers? Do we believe that miracles, whether understandable or not, are signs of God's work and activity?

Some scholars suggest that in some of the miracles of Jesus the miraculous element is rather 'mathematical'. By that they mean that, just as when a line intersects another line the divergence increases as the lines extend, so some of the miracles might have gained more drama as they were retold. They point to stories like Legion (Mark 5: 1–10), which in Matthew's account becomes two men (Matthew 8: 28). Another example occurs in what appears to be Matthew's repeat of Mark's story of blind Bartimaeus at Jericho (Mark 10: 46 and Matthew 20: 30), where two blind men are healed. So they wonder whether it could be that in stories like the Calming of the Tempest (Mark 4: 35–41), for example, the miracle was originally not so startling, but became more sensational as the story was repeated by various story-tellers. A kind of miracle 'inflation', so to speak!

It is an idea to be thought about, but a track which has to be trodden with great care, because there are many pitfalls and pot-holes along it. There is a delicate distinction between trying to magnify the miracles too much, as some people do, and trying to reduce them to the rudimentary and routine.

CHAPTER 4 (cont.)

vv. 35–41 The calming of the storm (Power over nature)

The name 'Galilee' comes from a word meaning 'circle' and in New Testament days there was a circle of towns around the lake. The lake itself was called 'Chinnereth' in the Old Testament (Numbers 34: 11) from the word for 'harp' and this no doubt referred to its shape. It is about 21 kilometres long and about 11 kilometres wide at its broadest point. Sometimes it is known as 'Gennesaret' (Luke 5: 1) from the plain along its north-west shores. It is also known as 'the sea of Galilee', and 'the sea of Tiberias' (John 6: 1) from the town on the lake-side named after the Roman Emperor Tiberias Caesar. This is the only inhabited town on the shores of the lake today.

Not surprisingly, with such a difficult story, there are many points of view regarding this miracle.

1. Many people, of course, accept it as it stands and see no reason why they should not, but somebody sooner or later will try to tell you that this was no miracle at all! They will point out that the lake is more than 180 metres below sea-level and in the hot climate the air sometimes rises very quickly, cold air comes in underneath, and the water is whipped up into a 'storm'. I myself have seen this happen. Then, as quickly as it rises, it stops. But consider, this would make the disciples out to be fools, not recognizing such a storm which they must have experienced before, and it would make Jesus an imposter and pretender.

2. Some think the rebuke of Jesus – 'be still, be muzzled' – was merely addressed to the terrified disciples, whose behaviour was threatening to sink the boat, and this coincided with the tempest dying down. So it was seen as Jesus speaking to the elements as well as to the disciples.

3. Others see the story as more of a parable than a miracle, with the disciples being content to let Jesus sleep and to do without him as long as the sky was blue and the sea was calm, then calling on him to save them when they thought they were going to die. This is certainly how some people treat God today. It should also be noted that the Jews thought of the sea, or 'the deep' as they called it, as the home of demonic powers, which Jesus here overcame.

Whatever we may think about it, it would certainly have been a story of great comfort to the early persecuted Christians, who were often in great danger themselves.

CHAPTER 5

vv. 1–20 Legion, the lunatic (Power over mental illness)

This is a very vivid story but difficult to understand. It is not easy to pin-point the place where it happened. Some manuscripts read 'Gerasenes', some 'Gadarenes', while some scholars think it was 'Gergesenes' because the area of Gergesa had a steep cliff overhanging the lake.

The person Tombs were often thought to be the haunts of evil spirits and mad people, so it was not surprising that Legion was thought to be mad and possessed with demons. He was a sad, wild, pathetic person who had been treated with scorn and cruelty by the local people. They had tried to tame him by chaining him down, which was the worst possible remedy, and no doubt they threw stones at him and called him names. Probably some parents told their children that 'old Legion' would have them if they didn't behave themselves.

What had caused him to be unbalanced? Possibly something the Romans had done to him or to his family (that is why he repeated the name Legion: an actual Roman legion numbered about 6000 men). Perhaps he had seen the word 'legion' on a tomb. Obviously the poor man believed himself to be possessed by 'many devils'.

When Jesus asked him his name he was gaining the man's confidence: to give your name in those days meant that you gave an indication of your personality to the questioner. He begged Jesus not do what everyone else seemed to do – torment him or send him away. Jesus effected a cure by convincing the man that the demons had transferred themselves into the pigs, who were already stampeding madly because of Legion's running about, and were now drowned. It seems to be a good example of Jesus the psychologist, as well as the exorcist.

Today we still speak of people who follow one another madly to a bad end as 'Gadarene swine', and when we sing the hymn 'Dear Lord and Father of mankind' we remember how Legion was 'reclothed and in his rightful mind' (v. 15).

After the cure the man naturally wanted to go with Jesus, probably out of gratitude and also because he would feel safe with someone who had helped him so much. But Jesus asked him to do a very difficult thing – to go back to his own people, who had dismissed him as a madman and an outcast, and show them what God had done for him.

DISCUSSION TOPICS

1. There is a great deal of mental illness and breakdown in our modern society. What are its possible causes and is there adequate provision for the treatment of the mentally ill?

2. In missionary work why is it often easier to go abroad than to stay in our

own neighbourhood? What is the reason for sending missionaries abroad when our own country is so much in need of the Christian gospel?

vv. 21–43 'Get up, little girl' (Power over death)
The place Probably Capernaum, though this is not certain.

The people Jairus, ruler or lay-president of the local synagogue: usually a dignified and rather distant figure, but right now he was a desperate man with a dangerously ill twelve-year-old daughter and he pleaded with Jesus to come and heal her. Note that it was not just to *see* her, but to *heal* her. Such was his faith in Jesus.

v. 24 *The crowd and the crush* Narrow streets, donkeys, baskets, barrows, everyone pushing everyone else – Jesus was so hemmed in he could hardly move. (A little like today when someone famous has a 'walkabout' and everyone tries to get near them.)

vv. 25–34 The interruption: the woman in the crowd (Power over physical illness)
Jesus stopped and said, 'Who touched me?' In a crowd like that! Wasn't that a silly question? No, he was conscious that someone had touched him, not by accident but out of real need. Power had gone from him. Who was it?

The poor woman had had some kind of haemorrhages for a long time – twelve years (the same as the age of the girl) – and nobody could cure her. She had no money because she had spent it all on doctors. (Note that when Luke tells this story (8: 43) he misses out the bit about doctors because, being one himself, he saw that as a slur on the profession!) But the woman had a lot of faith: she believed that if only she could touch Jesus's clothes she would be cured. Jesus told her that her faith had cured her, but he was also aware that 'power had gone out of him', so this incident seems to be a combination of faith-healing and someone being filled with a new strength just by touching his clothes.

In the gospels we are never told what Jesus looked like, e.g. whether he was tall or short, but the writers often tell us how he looked at people. He must have had the sort of eyes that looked at someone penetratingly and from whose gaze it was impossible to hide. The woman seems to have felt this because she 'trembled with fear' when Jesus looked at her. (See also Luke 22: 61, where Jesus looked at Peter.)

Throughout the centuries of Christianity people have tried to imagine what Jesus might have looked like since no genuine portrait or likeness of him is known to exist, although some now claim that the image of a face on the Shroud of Turin may provide that. The earliest likeness we have comes from a very faded wall-painting on the ceiling of a tomb in the catacombs of Rome, but there is no proof that this is authentic, although it is known that it was painted as early as about A.D. 150. A copy of this painting was made in 1847 by Thomas Heaphy and is now in the British Museum, but it is by no means certain that this copy closely resembles the original. It is an interesting piece of research to look at as many paintings of Jesus as possible and to see how he has been portrayed. Personally, I wonder why so many artists seem to regard him as being serious and sad. Bearing in mind that he had a keen sense of humour, as some of his parables make clear, why not depict him sometimes with a smile?

Two contrasting portraits of Jesus
Mosaic at Hosios Loukas monastery in Greece (11th century)

The Yellow Christ (1889), Paul Gauguin

v. 35 *The message* The woman was now much better, but Jairus's daughter was much worse. In fact, the messengers came to tell him that she had just died. Can you imagine his reaction to the news? He probably rounded on Jesus and said in frustration and sorrow, 'If only you had hurried up and not bothered with that woman. She could have waited until you came back, wasting time like that. Now it is too late.' I imagine him sitting down by the roadside and putting his head in his hands and then Jesus putting his arm around Jairus's shoulder and saying, 'It isn't too late. Don't worry, just have faith.'

It is easy, of course, to say that the girl was not really dead, only in some kind of coma, and that Jesus meant it literally when he said, 'She is only asleep'. But the hired mourners were already at their work, so they obviously assumed that the girl was dead, and they laughed at Jesus when he said that she was not. So he did not argue with them, he just pushed them all out and allowed into the room only the child's parents and the three favoured disciples. Mark tells us the actual Aramaic words Jesus used and gives the translation, probably for the benefit of his Greek readers. It is a very affectionate phrase, literally meaning 'little lamb get up', and it shows Jesus's great concern and love for the child.

Having just discussed how Jesus *looked* at people it is now worth thinking about Jesus's *hands*. In this incident he literally 'took her hands in his hands' and we can imagine that they were strong masculine hands, yet very gentle and sensitive. The power of healing flowed through his hands and the Church has always attached a lot of importance to the 'laying on of hands' in healing and blessing.

Note (v. 43) the request for secrecy about the matter. This is another example of what we call the 'Messianic secret'.

CHAPTER 6

vv. 1–6   What went wrong?
So far Mark has told only of Jesus's local journeys in and around Galilee – what we might call the 'Galilean ministry' or 'phase 1'. Now, in Chapters 6, 7 and 8 he tells of 'phase 2' – the more extensive travelling of Jesus outside Galilee, including Tyre and Sidon in Phoenicia, and up to Caesarea Philippi. Some scholars call this 'the flight from Galilee' and they point out that it follows this story of apparent rejection at Nazareth and the feeding of the five thousand when, as John tells us (6: 15), the people wanted Jesus to become their leader but Jesus refused.

We can assume that this incident happened at Nazareth, for Mark calls it 'his home town', although the word he used – 'patris' – often meant 'birthplace'. Does this mean that Mark thought of Nazareth as Jesus's birthplace and does it explain his silence about the birth at Bethlehem?

The synagogue was packed for the service (v. 2), which indicates Jesus's popularity as a preacher, but this seems to be the last sermon he gave in this way; afterwards, according to Mark at least, he preached in the open air.

Verse 3 is important because of its possible translations. Some read, 'Is not this the carpenter?' while others have, 'Is not this the son of the carpenter and Mary?' From this sole reference to Jesus's occupation we assume that he followed the trade of his father, as most Jewish boys did. But Geza Vermes, in his book *Jesus the Jew*, reminds us that in certain sayings of the Talmud, the later 'Book of Learning' in Jewish literature, the Aramaic noun denoting 'carpenter' could also mean 'scholar' or 'learned man'. Whether such a meaning of the word was current in Jesus's time we do not know for sure, but if so, the idea of Jesus as the local village craftsman may be inadequate.

In addition, some scholars point out that if we accept the reading 'the carpenter, the son of Mary', which is the usual translation, it may mean that Joseph, because he is not mentioned, had died. Also, to mention only a man's mother in those days was often to cast doubt on the identity of his father. So does this give us any clue to Mark's reluctance to write about the Virgin Birth?

Verse 3 also names Jesus's brothers and tells of his sisters, if we take the word in that family sense. James, 'the Lord's brother', became a leader of the church in Jerusalem, according to the Acts of the Apostles, and there are letters in the New Testament by James and Jude, who appear to be these men mentioned here.

This story is sometimes described as 'the rejection at Nazareth', but it was really an indifference on the part of the people. They were not saying, 'We know you as you really are, so we don't take any notice of you.' They just could not see any further than the mere man they had grown up with and knew as the local carpenter's son. They could not see his greatness and the meaning of his life. They knew his voice but not his vocation. They knew *about* him but did not really *know* him. It was not Jesus who failed, it was the people who failed to understand. They had asked the right questions but had come to the wrong conclusions.

There is a similar instance, and possibly the same one, described in Luke 4, although he gives us important additional information about the things that Jesus said in the synagogue.

vv. 7–13 Marching orders

Now it was the disciples' turn to try missionary work. They were to go and preach, teach and heal, in that order. Mark gives only a brief summary of the mission; Matthew 10 and Luke 9 and 10 give us more details. They were not going to be away for long and their equipment was to be the simplest. They had to travel light and to take the 'light' of Jesus's teaching with them. Money and food were not important. They went about in twos, probably for safety reasons but also because it was the practice of missionaries in the early Church. People who come to our doors today representing different religious sects often come in twos. The anointing of the sick with oil was also a custom of the early Church and many years later became known as the sacrament of holy unction.

vv. 14–29 How John lost his life

Mark has told us (1: 14) that John the Baptist had been put in prison. Now he tells us the reason for that and the story of John's death. Jesus's fame as a preacher and healer had spread and Herod – called by Mark 'King', but really only a tetrarch or ruler – assumed that John had come back to life. It was not uncommon in those days to believe that the spirit of a dead person could live again in the body of another person. Having quoted Herod as admitting that he had beheaded John, Mark explains how this came about.

The place According to Josephus, the Jewish historian, John was imprisoned in the fortress of Machaerus near the Dead Sea.

The occasion Herod's birthday party.

The people Mark seems a little confused here. It was not the wife of his brother Philip the tetrarch whom Herod had taken, but the wife of his half-brother, Herod Philip. Herodias was also 'King' Herod's niece, which made the complications – and the crime – even worse!

The protest If the brother were still alive and Herodias had been divorced, Herod could not marry her (Leviticus 18: 16; 20: 21). If he were dead, the marriage would not be lawful because there was a child (Deuteronomy 25: 5), although the law actually said that there must be no son and did not mention daughters. However, although Mark seems a bit confused, John the Baptist was very clear about *his* position. He didn't care whether Herod was a king or a mere commoner, he made his protest. His protest and his courage were to cost him his life.

DISCUSSION TOPIC

Some present-day protests do not cost much in terms of real sacrifice. Are they really worth very much? Note that Herod went 'in awe' of John (v. 20): he could not help but admire John's courage, but he could not match it.

The dancer She is not named in any of the gospels, but Herodias did have a daughter named Salome, so presumably this was the girl who danced. Artists and film-makers have often portrayed her as a seductive dancer of the 'seven veils' but I wonder whether this is in fact doing her a great injustice. Had she been a girl like that, can you imagine her, on being offered jewels, clothing, up to half a kingdom, running to her mother and asking what she should do? Wouldn't she have made up her own mind? It could be said that her mother was very dominating or even that Salome was a bit simple, but I believe she was a young girl who danced very prettily and in childlike innocence, and was used by her scheming mother to get revenge on John. For a mature princess to have danced in this way before a group of men would have seemed most degrading. Whatever the explanation, a brave man had lost his life. Herod was 'greatly distressed' (v. 26) but his pride and his fear of losing popularity outweighed any moral scruples he might have had. This is often the case with people in a similar dilemma.

It is strange that Luke does not mention this story.

vv. 30–44 The marvellous meal

The story of the feeding of the five thousand is the only miracle to be recorded in all four gospels. Some people find this surprising, but others see it as an indication of the importance all the gospel writers placed on this event.

The place This is uncertain. It is described as 'lonely' and was reached by boat so it was across the lake. Today the event is associated with a place called Tabgha and on the floor of the church there is a mosaic of the loaves and the fishes. What *is* certain is that Jesus desperately needed to get away for a rest. Mark says, 'He had no chance even to eat', which again shows the pressure that Jesus was under.

The people To get a full picture one has to build up the story from all four gospels. Mark tells of 'the green grass', John says it was Passover time, so it was in the spring. They all say there were five thousand men, Matthew adding 'besides women and children'. Only Philip asked about the cost of feeding all the people and only John tells us about Andrew bringing forward the boy who gave his five barley loaves and two fishes to Jesus.

The miracle Not surprisingly it has not lacked 'explanations'.

1. Some say it was not a miracle at all, just a boy sharing his sandwiches and everyone else, shamed by his unselfishness, doing the same. The result was a gigantic 'faith tea' with plenty left over. This sounds most improbable, because for one thing it was now very late in the day and it is most unlikely that they would all have had food to spare. But even at that level, in a part of the world always on the verge of famine, such sharing would have been a miracle and one that we would do well to copy today, in a world where there is so much hunger because of a refusal to share the earth's resources.
2. Some say Jesus was only doing what Moses had done in the wilderness (Exodus 16: 15). It is also a little like the story of Elisha (2 Kings 4: 42) feeding a hundred men with bread.
3. Others think it was a fulfilment of Isaiah 25: 6 – the Jewish idea of a Messianic banquet.
4. To some the 'breaking of the bread' (v. 41) is an anticipation of the Last Supper and the Holy Sacrament of the Church.
5. Others see this as Jesus demonstrating that he was the 'Bread of Life', satisfying people's deepest needs.
6. Some scholars look at the 'left-overs' and say that these symbolize not only the fact that everyone was satisfied, but also 'the truths that are always left when all else has been eaten'.

For me, however, the most important thing is not the miracle (I take that as it stands and do not see why not) but the picture of Jesus this story portrays. There were five thousand men (ordinary working men, most of them) so determined to talk to Jesus that they followed him probably quite a long way to that lonely place. Most of them had no doubt taken time off work to do so. What did they talk about? What was so interesting to them that they forgot about time and about food? Was it religion? Partly, perhaps, but not all day, surely. I would think they also talked about things like the political situation, the state of the nation, social problems, the Roman occupation and so on.

Who were these men? Notice how they sat down: Mark says in ranks of fifties and hundreds. Probably that is how they were counted: a hundred ranks of fifty equals five thousand.

It sounds like some kind of organization. Was there such an organization in Galilee? Yes, the Zealots, a very patriotic underground movement pledged to fight the Romans.

But who could have told them about Jesus? Remember, one of the disciples was Simon the Zealot.

What did they want with Jesus? John (6: 15) has the answer: 'They would have taken him by force and made him their king, or leader.' If this reckoning is right these men saw the *real* Jesus, not a stained-glass-window saint. They saw an intelligent, humorous, brave young man and they liked his brand of religion. They saw in this man an ideal leader to solve their political and social problems and perhaps lead them in a rebellion against Rome.

And that is exactly why Jesus turned the job down. It must have been quite a temptation, like the temptation to be a political Messiah (Luke 4: 5–8), but Jesus knew this was not the way. Revolution and violence can never succeed. His rule must be by love, not by force. So he sent the people away and went up into the hills to pray. It had been a very tense and tempting day but Jesus had won. By doing so, however, he had lost a lot of popularity.

vv. 45–52   Walking on the water

Again, many explanations are offered, such as Jesus walking *by* the water rather than *on* it, or that the disciples were nearer to land than they thought, and Jesus walked through the shallow water to the boat. Others see it as some kind of resurrection appearance which has been put back in time in the gospels. But all this reduces the incident to the trivial; the fact remains that the disciples were undoubtedly frightened and Jesus came to them in their distress, which would be a great comfort story to Mark's readers.

vv. 53–56   This is another example of the ministry we know little about.

CHAPTER 7

vv. 1–23 Personal pollution

Yet another argument with the Pharisees – this time it was over the washing of hands before a meal. It had nothing to do with hygiene – to wash one's hands before a meal for that reason is common sense – but this was for religious reasons. To the Jews, food was a gift from God and a meal was a time of friendship and fellowship. It was also a way of 'coming to God' and to do so one had to have 'clean hands'. By this strict washing of hands any pollution or defilement from contact with non-Jews was washed off before eating. Thus it was more a matter of consecration than of cleanliness. There were many ways in which a strict Jew could become 'defiled', e.g. by touching a tomb, a dead body, a leper, meat from an 'unclean' animal (of which there were many) and especially by contact with a gentile. All these things meant that their hands were polluted and such uncleanness had to be washed off before a meal could be eaten.

Jesus reminded the Pharisees how people got around the law when they wanted to. For example, the law said that a man must look after his parents, but if he did not want to, he would give the money to the temple or to charity and would then say, 'I would like to help but my money has been given away' (or at least promised, because 'Corban' means 'sacred gift' or 'devoted to God'). Then Jesus told them what really defiled a person. It is not what we eat or how we wash, although obviously we should be sensible about these things, it is what we *think*. It is evil thoughts that lead to evil actions. Note, in vv. 21 and 22, the way in which Jesus groups major and minor sins together, like a poison register. We may well pride ourselves that we steer clear of the worst kinds of sin, but others, like envy, malice, arrogance, are not so easy to avoid. Real religion is in the heart, not worn on the sleeve.

vv. 24–30 The daughter and the dogs

The place   The Phoenician town of Tyre (where Jezebel came from). This is the beginning of the journeys outside Galilee.

Why did Jesus go there?   Either to try to 'get away from it all' for a rest, or to avoid being seen in Galilee after the five-thousand incident.

The woman   'Syro-Phoenician' because she was born in Phoenicia and lived in the province of Syria, or perhaps she was of mixed parentage. 'Clementine' literature (so-called because it is believed to have been written by Clement, Bishop of Rome, in about A.D. 100) says she was named Justa and that her daughter was Bernice. Some versions say she was a Greek, possibly because she spoke that language. Matthew (15: 22) says she was a 'Canaanite', i.e. descended from an old Canaanite tribe. He also omits the part about Jesus going into a foreigner's house.

Again, this is a story which Luke omits and in this case it seems very strange since one of Luke's intentions was to show Jesus's concern for foreigners.

The conversation   How she found Jesus is not clear, but the conversation was cutting. Some preachers maintain that Jesus was being rude to her but that would have been completely out of character on his part. Some Jews called foreigners 'dogs', meaning scavengers, while they thought of themselves as 'the children', so perhaps Jesus was reminding this woman of what some Jews would have said to her, a foreigner. On the other hand, perhaps he was testing her, or even teasing her a bit. After all, he was desperately in need of rest and quiet, and she could have been just an inquisitive neighbour. However, her ready wit and sense of humour was her saving grace and Jesus did as she asked. Of course, we must also remember that the whole story may have been a bit exaggerated by those who resented the foreign woman's intrusion. In fact, Matthew portrays Jesus as being almost reluctant to help the woman, but I prefer Mark's version of the story. In any case the word used here for 'dog' is not a derogatory term. (There were two Greek words for 'dog'; the one Jesus used meant a domesticated dog rather than a scavenger.) Jesus cured the woman's daughter (one of the few examples of healing from a distance) but it cost him his attempt at a holiday and he had to go back to Galilee.

vv. 31–37   A deaf and dumb man

This is one of two healing miracles found only in Mark; the other one is the blind man (8: 22). Here Mark's geography seems to be wrong, for Sidon is about 40 kilometres *up* the coast from Tyre – a very strange way of getting back to Galilee! Perhaps by 'Sidon' he meant 'Saida', because if we leave off 'Beth' ('house of') from 'Bethsaida' the two words are very similar in the Hebrew text. For Jesus to have gone via Bethsaida would have made much more sense.

The use of spittle was a very ancient remedy for the eyes. Note that Mark again gives the Aramaic word that Jesus used and then translates it.

Request for secrecy   Why did Jesus so often ask people to keep quiet about the miracles he performed? It was really a question of secrecy about 'Messiahship' – the Messianic secret. Jesus was anxious not to be thought of as just a healer or a popular Messiah. In addition, to some Jews the word 'Messiah' meant a political leader and to the Romans the word indicated some kind of revolutionary. Jesus was not that kind of Messiah and he was most anxious to play down such ideas, but after these miracles of healing there was little chance of secrecy being maintained. Note the compliment to Jesus in v. 37: 'All that he does, he does well.'

CHAPTER 8

vv. 1–10   Feeding the four thousand

Isn't this the same story as the feeding of the five thousand?
Some scholars think it is, pointing out that the Bible does duplicate stories

sometimes and that in the original Greek some words are common to both stories. However, there are more differences than a mere retelling of the same story could justify. In any case in vv. 19 and 20 Jesus refers to both events.

The occasion and the meaning of this story seem to me to be very different from the feeding of the five thousand. For example, the number seven was very significant for the Jews: the Sabbath was the seventh day; the seventh year was the sabbatical year for the fields, i.e. no crops were grown; a seven-branched candlestick was used in the tabernacle in the wilderness (Exodus 25: 37). Then later, in the Acts of the Apostles (6: 3), seven men were chosen to look after the gentile interests, so some scholars see this feeding as a 'bridge' between Jew and gentile, with Jesus offering the 'bread of life' to the outsiders just as he had offered it to the Jews. Personally, I think we might look for a much simpler explanation, such as Jesus feeling 'sorry for the people' (v. 2) because they were poor and hungry.

vv. 11–21 Fears and fermentations

The Pharisees wanted 'a sign', some kind of proof that Jesus was what people were saying he was – the Messiah. What the Pharisees had seen and heard already was not, apparently, enough to convince them, which was a sign of their own blindness! Jesus refused to give such evidence: they would probably not accept it if he did. This leads Mark on to the subject of the influence of the Pharisees – the 'yeast'. This foments as well as ferments, i.e. it is a corruptive influence as well as a raising agent. So the Pharisees' influence was bad because they had no real perception of Jesus's work, though neither for that matter had the disciples (v. 21). (It is worth noting, however, that Mark often seems deliberately to undermine the disciples' ability to understand.)

vv. 22–26 The blind man of Bethsaida

The place is sometimes called 'Bethsaida Julius' in honour of Julia, the daughter of the Emperor Augustus. This is one of the two miracles found only in Mark. (The other is the healing of the deaf and dumb man in Chapter 7.) The healing was not immediate, but in stages. The man said he could see people 'like trees', which probably meant that he could see people carrying bundles of sticks on their backs, as they did in those days, and they would look like moving bushes. It could be argued, perhaps, that this miracle was also an acted parable: Jesus had just been talking to the disciples about not being able to see what he meant (v. 18), now he was helping a blind man to see gradually and slowly until he could 'see everything plainly and distinctly' (v. 25). Again (v. 26) there is the request for secrecy.

Places like Bethsaida and Capernaum were only villages. Why is there no reference to Jesus visiting cities, apart from Jerusalem?
This raises some interesting points. In the synoptic gospels Jesus is not only a man of Galilee, but of *rural* Galilee. His parables and his teaching rarely reflect city life. There is no mention, for example, of him ever going to

Sephoris, one of the chief cities of Galilee and only 6½ kilometres from Nazareth, or to Tiberias, a very important city on the lake-side. Of course, some of the references to his travels, e.g. Mark 6: 56, indicate that he visited bigger towns and certainly Jesus was well aware of many of the problems of city life, but it does seem that whenever possible he sought the silence of the countryside and the open air, away from the clamour of the city streets.

vv. 27–38   You are the Christ!

This is often known as 'Peter's confession'. We are now just half-way through this gospel and this incident is the turning-point of Mark's record.

The place   On the way to Caesarea Philippi (named after Caesar and Philip, brother of Herod Antipas and son of Herod the Great), some 40 kilometres north of Galilee. The Greek nature god Pan (of the 'Pipes of Pan' legend) had been worshipped there at one time, hence its old name of Paneas. Today it is known as Baneas and attracts visitors who wish to see the source of the River Jordan nearby.

The question   'Who do people think I am?'
This shows Jesus's concern over the attitude of the people of Galilee towards his ministry. The Jewish idea of a Messiah was based on Old Testament passages like those in Isaiah 9 and 11 – a political, nationalistic figure, setting up a kingdom on earth, defeating enemies and bringing a time of peace. Jesus's idea of a Messiah was very different. It was based on Isaiah 53 – the 'suffering servant', a very complicated concept, but basically embodying the belief that to suffer and to sacrifice brings greater victory than does force of arms. Jesus was anxious to discover what impression he had made on ordinary people.

The answer   The disciples told him that people thought of him as John the Baptist or Elijah or one of the prophets, which was a typical traditional Old Testament kind of response. If this was the case and this misunderstanding widespread, then Jesus realized that such impressions would have reached the ears of Herod and he might well want to put an end to Jesus's ministry, as he had done to that of John the Baptist.

What about you?   Impulsive Peter told him, 'We think you are the Messiah'. The word 'Messiah' was Hebrew for 'anointed one'. The Greek word was 'Christos', from which we get the English word 'Christ'. This was the first time anyone had actually called Jesus 'the Messiah', so it was a turning-point in his ministry. Again he gave them strict orders to keep quiet about it (v. 30). Then came the bombshell: he told them that he was going to suffer and die (v. 31).

Peter was astounded and horrified. Hadn't Jesus just admitted, or at least he had not denied, that he was the Messiah? Such a Messiah would surely be victorious, a king, bringing in a new age, so what was all this about dying and defeat? It didn't make sense, so Peter took Jesus aside and remonstrated with him.

Then came the second shock. Jesus turned to Peter and said, 'Get away from me, Satan (tempter). You have got it wrong. I am not that kind of Messiah.'

After that Jesus made clear to them what he meant. Those who would follow him must be prepared to suffer and to sacrifice. It may mean being prepared to die, but it also means being prepared to *live* for Christ and that is sometimes more difficult. It does not mean going about with a long face and looking as if we have all the trouble in the world, although some Christians seem to think that. It means putting self to death – becoming truly unselfish – because selfishness is the main cause of so much sin. The way to real freedom is to break out of the prison of self-centredness, self-interest and self-indulgence, then we are free to serve others. Service means self-sacrifice and sometimes suffering.

Matthew 16 makes important additions to this story (e.g. Jesus says, 'Who do men say the Son of Man is?'), chiefly the words to Peter, 'You are the rock and on this rock I will build my church'. This was a play on words: the name 'Petros', from the Greek 'petra', meant rock or stone, so did the Aramaic 'Kephas' or 'Cephas'. Christians differ in their interpretations of these words. Some say that Jesus meant Peter the man and on him he would build the Church, making Peter its first leader or bishop. Others believe that Jesus was referring to Peter's faith and insight in recognizing Jesus as the Messiah, while others think that he meant the kind of character Peter was to develop later on. The word 'church' is used in the gospels only twice – here and in Matthew 18: 17.

There is a similar story in Jewish literature about a king who wanted to build a palace but found only soft sand until he dug down to a rock and on that he built his palace. It also sounds a little like the parable of the two houses at the end of the Sermon on the Mount (Matthew 7: 25).

CHAPTER 9

vv. 2–8   The transfiguration

What does the word mean?   'Change of appearance'.

The place   Probably on or near to Mount Hermon, a snow-capped peak 2700 metres high, 22 kilometres north of Caesarea Philippi (although Mount Tabor in Galilee is also a possibility).

The time   Six days after Peter's confession. (Luke says eight days.) In that time Jesus *could* have travelled down to Mount Tabor.

The people   The usual three disciples, Peter, James and John. Jesus, whose garments are described as 'dazzling white', is joined by Moses and Elijah.

How did the disciples know it was Moses and Elijah? Probably from their ideas of these men from the Old Testament.

What did it all mean? Many explanations have been given or attempted, but the central fact is that Moses represented the Jewish law, or Torah, while Elijah represented the prophets and prophecy. The Jewish religion was built on these two things. Then the voice from heaven (the second occasion it is heard) said, 'This is my Son; listen to *Him*'; in other words, 'He is the authority greater than the law or the prophets, and the greatest law-giver and prophet of all. Pay attention to what he says.' It was God confirming what Peter had said – that Jesus was the Christ.

The cloud (the word in Hebrew is 'shekina') was the symbol of the presence of God (Exodus 40: 34). Another link between this story and Moses is the account of Moses coming down from the mountain (Exodus 34: 29) with his face 'shining so much that it had to be covered with a veil'.

Notice Jesus's request for secrecy about all this. On the way down the disciples questioned him about this 'rising from the dead' because they could not understand what he meant.

vv. 14–29 Down to earth

From the mountain top to the mundane – the work was waiting for Jesus. The boy suffered from epilepsy, which was seen in those days as being 'possessed by demons'. This is not a very good example of healing through faith, in fact the father *lacked* faith.

QUESTIONS

Did Jesus believe in 'possession by demons' or did he have to heal in the only way that people could understand? To what extent was he a man of his time, sharing contemporary ideas?

These are difficult questions. My personal opinion is that he was to a certain extent bounded by his humanity and therefore by time and place, but he was bringing to bear healing power which knew no bounds or limitations. You might say that he was bounded by the language which he spoke but his teaching is for all time and for all people. In v. 19 Jesus sounds a bit tired and even impatient, which is not surprising considering the ineffectiveness of the disciples and the hostility of the authorities, but he was not too tired or troubled to heal the boy. The father's cry from the heart, 'I have some faith but help me where my faith falls short', is a plea with which many people can sympathize.

It is worth noting Jesus's impatience here. I think we have to accept that the 'Gentle Jesus, meek and mild' picture is a bit overplayed. Indeed, it can give a completely false impression of Jesus. He *was* gentle – all really great people are – but his meekness was never weakness and he could at times get angry. Not bad-tempered, that is a weakness, but righteous indignation is part of a strong personality. It all depends, as we have said, on what a person gets angry about and how they express that anger.

vv. 30–32 This is Jesus's second warning about his approaching death, and there seems to be the same inability or reluctance on the part of the disciples to understand what he meant. When we do not want to accept something it is amazing how 'blind and deaf' we can become.

vv. 33–37 The least shall be the greatest

This is the last time that Capernaum is mentioned in Mark's gospel. Jesus was now on his way to Jerusalem for the Passover and the disciples had been arguing along the road about who was the greatest or the most important of them. Probably they had been discussing the coming kingdom, thinking it would be an earthly kingdom set up in Jerusalem, and they wanted top jobs in it. 'If you want to be important,' said Jesus, 'then be prepared to make yourself a servant', which is not advice many people want to take. It seems to be a contradiction in terms, being a servant and being great, but if we look at the lives of really great people in the world what do we find common to them all? They all serve other people, often in a very lowly way.

vv. 38–41 'Closed shops' and cups of water

This is the only time in the synoptic gospels that the disciple John speaks by himself and this little speech does not do him much credit, although it possibly sheds some light on why he was called a 'son of thunder' (3: 17). How many times in the history of religion have people been persecuted because they were not 'one of us' – not of our denomination, not of our belief, not a member of our church, and so on? It is a very narrow way of deciding what God's work is all about. People are also persecuted because of their colour, as well as their creed.

Jesus, as he so often did, brought it down to the basics. A cup of cold water may not seem much to us today, but in those days water was not only scarce but often regarded as sacred. It may well have meant the difference between life and death and was of far greater value than money. To give someone in need a life-giving drink was a deed of great goodness and often of sacrifice. It was better than the mere chanting of psalms in the synagogue or the tossing of a few coins into the offertory box in the temple.

v. 36 The child

He was used as an example, probably because in those days children were often thought of as unimportant. 'Let your greatness start by caring for children.' Think of all the Christian work done in caring for children and of the horrific examples of neglect and cruelty reported by, for example, the N.S.P.C.C. A nation can be judged by the way it treats its children.

Jesus drives home the point in v. 42: 'Those who cause little ones who have faith to stumble or go wrong would be better to be drowned in the sea.' (The millstone was a huge grinding stone pulled round by a donkey.) These are angry and measured words of Jesus and it is worth noting that they are directed against those who cause 'little ones' to go astray. There are many ways of causing young people to go wrong, and not only children, but those who are 'young in faith'. It is a good exercise to list and discuss some of them. Do we feel equally angry at the causes of stumbling in our society today?

vv. 43–48   Watch yourself! Cut it out!

In caring about offences against others, we must not forget offences against ourselves. Jesus, of course, is using vivid exaggeration here but the point is clear. Hands and eyes can be instruments of sinful acts, so he tells his listeners to *watch themselves* and to cut out the things that lead them into evil.

'Hell', or 'Hades' is a translation of the Greek word 'Gehenna', or Hebrew 'Ge Hinnom', a valley near Jerusalem where fire-worship of the god Molech was practised by King Ahaz in Old Testament times. The valley was also used for burning rubbish, so it came to be associated with the place of burning and punishment.

CHAPTER 10   ON THE WAY TO JERUSALEM

Mark is now moving towards the climax of his gospel. His readers wanted to know how, why and where Jesus died, and who was responsible for his death. Mark tells them by devoting a third of his gospel record to it. These chapters, 10–15, have been called 'the way of the cross', for obvious reasons. Chapter 10 tells of the travelling of Jesus and the disciples from the north down to Jericho and it is obvious that Mark condenses a journey which must have taken quite a long time.

vv. 2–12   Love and marriage

Here Jesus was being asked to decide between two rival schools of thought among the scribes. Followers of Rabbi Hillel said that divorce could be for very trivial reasons, like burning the bread. The school of Rabbi Shammai, however, maintained that divorce should be allowed only for adultery and indecency (see Deuteronomy 24: 1). (Shammai and Hillel were leaders of the two most important Pharisaic schools at this time.) A man obtained a divorce simply by giving his wife a note of dismissal and the marriage contract was then ended.

Divorce was easy too in permissive Roman society and Mark's readers would include some of these people, so they would be interested in Jesus's attitude towards marriage and divorce. They would have had an added interest because in Roman society there were signs, as far as certain women were concerned, of what we now call 'equal opportunity'. For example, if the husband committed adultery, the wife could not only sue for divorce but could also claim equal shares of any property and possessions. So the whole business was a burning issue, which had generated a lot of heat as well as some 'holy smoke' that had rather confused vital issues.

Jesus lifted the whole idea of marriage on to a higher plane by saying:
1. There must be equality between the man and the woman. In Jewish law only the man could divorce his wife; the woman was not permitted to divorce her husband. It was a man's world, but here Jesus was saying that women were people, not objects.
2. Marriage was a sacred thing, not a 'trial offer' or a 'money-back-if-not-satisfied' arrangement. Easy divorce and injustice were violations of what marriage was all about. It was not a matter of mere pleasure but of holy purpose. It is worth noting that Jesus's attitude to and treatment of women were always the same. A useful exercise is to make a list of all the incidents in which he came into contact with women of many types and backgrounds.

QUESTIONS

Was Jesus laying down a law about marriage for all time and all marriages? What is the main purpose of marriage? Did he mean that a man and woman should continue to live together even if they did not love each other? Is it not better for children to be parted from parents who are always quarrelling? What causes marriages to break up? Should the Church remarry divorced people? What about 'trial' marriages? What are the essential ingredients for a successful marriage? Is there a better expression of good human relationships than a happy marriage?

When sexual relationships are only for 'kicks', who gets hurt most? What are the consequences of regarding human beings as 'playthings' rather than as people? Why are there strong connections between pornography and crimes of violence?

The main consideration in all these questions must be human and moral values. I think history has proved that whenever families and marriage have been regarded as of little importance society as a whole has suffered. It has been described as God's arithmetic: 'one plus one equals one'.

vv. 13–16 Love and mercy

Following the discussion on marriage and family life Mark tells how children were brought to Jesus to be blessed.

Who were the 'they' who brought the children?   Probably their mothers.

Why were the disciples so touchy?   They probably thought that Jesus would not have the time for or want to bother with children. It is another example of Jesus having to rebuke the disciples.

It is said that one can tell a person's character from the things he gets really angry about. Jesus got angry about many things – hypocrisy, dishonesty, child-abuse, half-heartedness, callousness. It was never anger about wrongs done to *himself*, only to others. 'To receive the kingdom of God like a child' (v. 15) is to be receptive and responsive, and dependent on the things of God.

vv. 17–31   Love of money

This would-be disciple opened the discussion by asking Jesus about obtaining 'eternal life'. By that he meant a quality of life, life at its best, not life after death. Jesus said no one is good but God, which showed his humanity and humility.

At first sight it seems that this man would be a very suitable candidate: he had kept all the commandments from his boyhood, so he said. What a record breaker!

Then why didn't Jesus accept him?   Knowing human nature as he did, he quickly saw the young man's weakness: the keeping of the commandments had never really *cost* him anything. With his good home and wealthy parents he had never been tempted to steal, or defraud, or dishonour his parents, so Jesus asked him to go and do something that would really cost him something, and he couldn't do it. He loved his money and his comfortable life too much. (The fact that Jesus 'looked at him and loved him' (v. 21) makes some scholars think that he might have been the 'disciple whom Jesus loved' in John's gospel, but that seems improbable.)

If the man had gone off and sold his possessions and given all his money away, would he not then have become poor himself and become a burden on other people?

Not necessarily: St Francis of Assisi did just that and he didn't become a burden on anyone! However, this question of wealth (or 'the right use of money', as John Wesley called it) has always been a difficult one. We live in an age and in a society where money is spent – and sometimes wasted – in huge quantities on projects, pleasures and possessions which are often regarded as very questionable from a moral point of view. The idea of money as a talent, to be used properly and not abused, is not very fashionable. But to regard money in itself as evil, so that a poor person is regarded as pious and a rich one as a rogue, is wrong. Wealth can – and does – corrupt a person, and not only those who have it, but also those who become envious and resentful of such people. Greed and need are often confused and we would all be better off – in the real sense – if we thought more about our standard of *giving* than about our standard of *living*.

After the man had gone, Jesus talked to the disciples about money. What was Jesus's attitude towards wealth? It was not Jesus but Paul, writing to Timothy (1 Timothy 6: 10), who said that 'the love (or lust) of money is the root of all evil'. Jesus's attitude was that money can become something that uses *us*, rather than something that we use. It can give us a sense of false security, an illusion that money can buy anything or anybody, if they have loyalty or secrets to sell. It can become an object of worship and a main preoccupation of life. A person who cares too much about money is like Gulliver lying on the beach at Lilliput, bound by 'lots and lots of little strings'.

'The eye of the needle' (v. 25) was possibly a small gateway in the old wall of Jerusalem through which a laden camel could pass only with extreme difficulty. Alternatively, the original Greek word may have been 'cable', not 'camel' (some Greek manuscripts do use this word), or perhaps it was just another of Jesus's humorous exaggerations, taking the idea from an ancient proverb of an elephant trying to do a similar thing.

Impulsively Peter mentions the things they have given up to follow Jesus; he is told they will have their reward one day. Such words from Jesus would be of great comfort to the persecuted Christians to whom Mark was writing.

vv. 32–34 Here is the third warning about Jesus's imminent death, this time in more detail. He mentioned that Jerusalem was the place where it would all happen. Notice that Jesus walked on ahead, knowing what was going to happen yet never flinching from it, while the disciples stumbled on behind him.

vv. 35–45 'Do us a favour'
The nickname given to James and John was mentioned earlier (3: 17). It could have meant that they wanted to 'steal the thunder' by gaining honour and glory in the kingdom Jesus talked about. They had not paid much attention to Jesus's remarks about service and humility since they seemed to think that the kingdom was an earthly affair and they wanted top jobs in it. It was a complete misunderstanding of Jesus's teaching and he told them so, using two Old Testament ideas: the cup of suffering (Isaiah 51: 17–22) and the baptism of suffering (Isaiah 43: 2 and Psalm 42: 7). Verse 39 indicates that James and John became martyrs later. Verse 45 shows Jesus as the 'suffering servant' Messiah of Isaiah 53.

vv. 46–52 The blind beggar
I wonder whether Mark placed this incident after the query by James and John to emphasize their 'blindness'!

The place Jericho, a city down in the 'wilderness', near the Dead Sea. It is known as the 'city of palm trees' because it is built around an oasis where tropical fruit and trees grow. At almost 250 metres below sea-level, it is the lowest inhabited place on the earth's surface and almost certainly the oldest walled city that we yet know of. From there it was a very hard climb up to Jerusalem, about 25 kilometres up in the hills and 760 metres above sea-level.

The person Bartimaeus ('Bar' means 'son of'). Jesus had much on his mind, but he had time for a blind beggar at the roadside.

The miracle This is the last miracle in Mark's gospel. Imagine the heat, the excitement, the movement, as the crowd followed Jesus. Who cared about a blind beggar? Why didn't he just shut up and put up with being kicked around? However, Bartimaeus wanted better treatment than that and he shouted more loudly.

Was this a good example of faith? Not really. The beggar seemed more intent on shouting slogans at Jesus about being the 'Son of David', possibly thinking that Jesus would give him money for such flattery. He gave him far more than money, something that money could not buy. Jesus asked him what he really wanted and the answer was 'my sight'. Notice that although Bartimaeus shouted Messianic slogans Jesus made no request for secrecy. Perhaps he knew that soon the secret would be out in any case.

Houses below the Temple Mount, Jerusalem (reconstruction)

Chapters 11-15: The Last Week

These chapters in the synoptic gospels – for Luke (19–23) and Matthew (21–27) follow Mark – are concerned with the last week in the life of Jesus, often called 'Holy Week'. A summary of the week's events would be as follows:

Sunday	Palm Sunday
Monday	cleansing the temple
Tuesday	attempts to discredit Jesus
Wednesday	the anointing at Bethany
Thursday	a.m. preparation for the Last Supper
	p.m. the Last Supper
Friday	(very early) the arrest in Gethsemane
	the Jewish trial
	the Roman trial and the crucifixion
Saturday	the Sabbath
Sunday	the resurrection and Easter Day

This section of Mark's gospel was probably a standard text of the early church, which had been written down earlier and which formed the first block of his gospel, most likely copied from an earlier record. (Luke begins his gospel by referring to 'the many writers who have drawn up an account', so there must have been several other written records.) If this is so, then Mark's gospel was put together 'backwards', i.e. the rest of the account has been added on to this narrative of the last week.

Did Jesus visit Jerusalem only once?   This is one of the points on which the gospels differ, because John's gospel mentions several visits to Jerusalem. Is it likely that Jesus would visit the capital city only once? Did Mark condense into one week events which extended over a longer period and possibly involved more than one visit? Some scholars think he did. Some people even liken the six days of Holy Week to the six days of Creation, but not very convincingly. (The theory goes as follows. Mark probably expanded and amplified an earlier pre-Marcan narrative of the Passion, just as the writer of Genesis probably adapted an earlier account of Creation. There may well have been 'stages of growth' before Mark made the 'week' in Jerusalem the climax of his account. So, as with the Creation story, there is a day by day unfolding of the drama, with the climax being reached on the sixth day and the Sabbath being the rest after the events. It is all rather tenuous, but one is bound to wonder why Mark was so careful to slot the whole story, from Chapter 11 to Chapter 16, into such definite days. Luke does not seem to follow that pattern.)

CHAPTER 11

vv. 1–11   Day 1: Palm Sunday

The pilgrims, who were in Jerusalem for the festival of the Passover, which commemorated the Exodus from Egypt (Exodus 12), tore off branches from the palm trees along the road to strew in the path of Jesus as he rode on the donkey (no doubt to the cry of 'vandals' from some shocked householders along the route!): hence the name 'Palm Sunday'.

Why did the people get so excited? It was probably because they had in mind the prophecy of Zechariah (9: 9) about the king coming 'riding on an ass'. They really thought that at last, after many years, the prophecy was being fulfilled and their shouts were clearly Messianic (see Psalm 118: 26). They also remembered how kings in the Old Testament, such as David and Solomon, rode into Jerusalem on a white horse for their coronation. The trouble was that they all missed the point: Jesus was riding on a lowly beast of burden and peace, not on a war horse.

It is worth noting that this seems to be the only mention of Jesus riding anywhere although we can not assume that he never did so at other times. He travelled about a lot, often in wild and desolate countryside and in a hot climate, yet apparently he preferred to walk rather than ride. He must have been physically very fit to do this and it must have taken much longer to get from place to place than we may realize. The animal he rode here had never been ridden before, which probably meant that it was seen as suitable for a sacred purpose, just as an animal 'without blemish' would be used as a sacrifice. Perhaps Jesus now saw himself as the 'approaching sacrifice', as the Palm Sunday hymn 'Ride on, ride on in Majesty' puts it.

Who arranged all this? It seems as though Jesus himself did. He had apparently arranged for the colt to be there and had prepared a password for anyone who wanted to know what was going on. Perhaps he was now ready to reveal the Messianic secret – that he was the Messiah, but not the kind they were expecting. This was borne out by the fact that when the procession reached the city Jesus did nothing except look round the temple (v. 11); this would have been a great disappointment to those who thought he was going to start some kind of revolution or protest.

Is that why Judas offered to betray him? I think so. He did not do it for the money because the amount involved was not very great, or out of jealousy, or because he wanted to be the leader of the disciples, or for any of the other reasons some commentators or psychiatrists have put forward. I think he was a man who was a very strong nationalist or patriot and he badly wanted Jesus to prove himself to be the Messiah. So when Jesus rode into Jerusalem and then did nothing, Judas, in his frustration and disappointment, decided to put Jesus into such a position that he would be forced to act and to show himself as the Messiah. How better to do this than to get him arrested and then see some kind of dramatic miracle or rescue – a show of power which would reveal to everyone that he *was* the kind of Messiah they expected and wanted? And when Judas realized that Jesus was going to die rather than do that, he took the money back to the priests and said, 'I have betrayed an innocent man' (Matthew 27: 4) and then committed suicide.

That theory at least avoids the difficult theological complications of saying that Judas acted as he did because it was all foreordained and therefore he had no choice. In that case he would merely have been used and would therefore not have been responsible for his actions.

Day 2: Monday

vv. 12–14 The fig tree

This is a strange story. There are three possible explanations:

1. An actual miracle: this seems unlikely.
2. An acted parable: the fig tree represented Israel (as in the Old Testament, e.g. 1 Kings 4: 25 and Hosea 9: 10), which now bore 'no fruit' and no one would eat from it spiritually. This seems to be a more plausible explanation.
3. A reference to Bethphage, which means 'House of unripe figs'.

vv. 15–19 The temple protest

To call this incident 'the cleansing of the temple' is not quite accurate. Jesus did not go into the temple itself, that great white marble building begun by Herod the Great in 20 B.C. and which, according to John's gospel (2: 20), had taken forty-six years to build. (Since Solomon's temple had been destroyed by the Babylonians in 586 B.C. no real attempt had been made to replace it, except for the temple started, but probably never finished, by Zerubbabel, described in Ezra 3.) In Herod's building the actual temple, or sanctuary, stood on raised ground surrounded by a large precinct. Part of this open area was known as the 'Court of the Gentiles', and this division of the temple compound into two separate areas gives us a clue as to what Jesus was protesting about. There were three things:

1. Dishonesty

Jewish pilgrims from all over the ancient world, where they had been 'dispersed' or had gone to live, came to Jerusalem for the Passover. It was the first of three annual festivals at which all the men had to appear (Deuteronomy 16: 16). On arrival they had to give money to the temple offering and they also had to buy a sacrifice to take into the temple, whatever they could afford. In order to do these things they had to change any 'pagan' coins they had brought (i.e. those with a 'heathen' image on them which could not be taken into the temple) into Jewish currency. No doubt some of the money-changers gave short change or sold second-class sacrifices and this made Jesus angry. Using Jeremiah's phrase (Jeremiah 7: 11) when he had made his protest at Solomon's temple six hundred years earlier, Jesus said they were turning the temple into a 'den of thieves'. Of course not all the traders were cheats and in any case this matter of dishonesty was only part of his protest.

2. Desecration
It was not only the thieving, it was the fact that trading was taking place at all in a holy place. Jesus was protesting against the way in which God's house had been commercialized and used for purposes utterly unworthy of true worship. It was all being done in the name of religion and no doubt the religious leaders, who got high rents from the traders, said that it 'raised money for the temple', but Jesus regarded the whole matter as being seedy and sordid, with all the noise and the arguing and the litter. It needed a reminder of the prophecy of Malachi that 'the Lord would suddenly come to his temple like a refiner's fire' (Malachi 3: 1–3).

3. Discrimination
Worst of all was the fact that all this was going on in the gentile section, implying that that area was not very important as far as worship was concerned. People carrying shopping were even using it as a short cut. However, between that area and the Jewish temple proper was a barrier with a grim warning on it: 'Let no foreigner cross this barrier except on penalty of death'. Jesus was very angry at this kind of division and raising his voice, this time in the words of Isaiah (56: 7), he shouted, 'This house should be a house of prayer for *all* nations', i.e. not just for Jews.

So Jesus made his protest and, like John the Baptist before him, it was to cost him his life.

QUESTION

Would Jesus condemn some of the ways in which a number of churches raise money today?
I have a suspicion that at times he would. Obviously the churches concerned could not be accused of deception and no doubt their motives are sound, but the fact remains that some bazaars are a bit bizarre and some of the lotteries, though lucrative, can give the church a bad image. This is also true of certain investments and interests. The Church, like any other organization, needs money in order to do its work, but how the money is raised should be a matter of concern. One has to balance the fact that the money has been put to a good cause against a possible encouragement, for example, of gambling, which is a social problem the Church should be trying to combat, not condone.

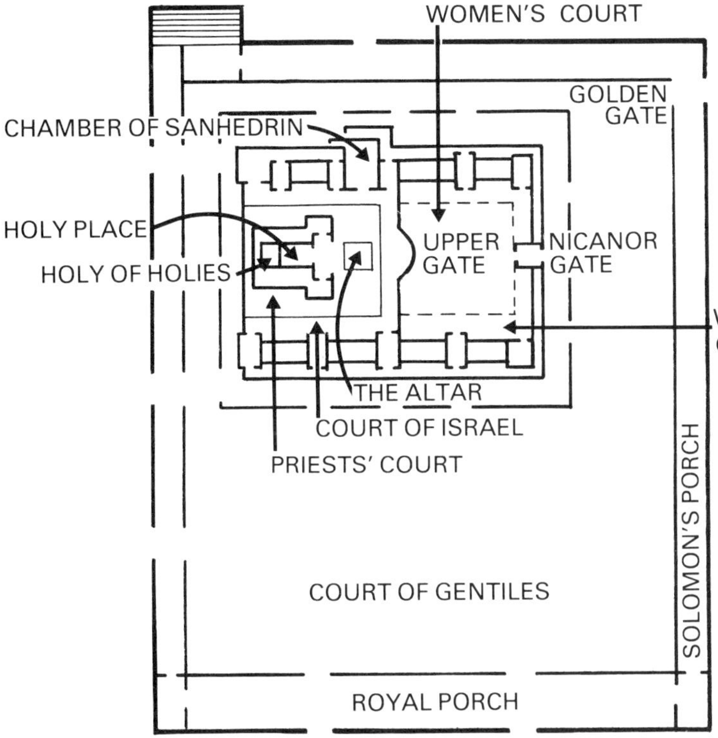

Plan of Herod's temple in Jerusalem

A model of the temple

vv. 20–25   **The fig tree withered**
Luke omits this incident and Matthew abridges it, almost as though they thought it was unworthy of Jesus, and I am inclined to agree with them. The tree had apparently died in the night. Peter's remark (v. 21) may have had some significance since Peter himself was to 'wither away' later in the week when he denied Jesus. Mark uses the incident to record a little collection of Jesus's sayings about faith, prayer, etc.

Day 3: Tuesday

The trick questions
Not surprisingly, the religious leaders were outraged by this 'cleansing of the temple'. Jesus had challenged their authority, he had become a menace and a danger to them, and they were determined that he should die. But how could they achieve this? His action had made him a popular hero: many people had wanted to do something about the trading in the temple courtyard but had not found the courage, so they admired someone who had. The religious leaders decided to try to discredit Jesus in the eyes of the people – to get him to say or do something which would show that he was not such a hero after all. They thought up some questions to trap him.

vv. 27–33   **'Who gave you permission to do this?' (They were referring to the 'cleansing of the temple'.)**
If he had said, 'No one', they would have said that he acted unlawfully. If he had said, 'By God's authority', they would have said it was blasphemy. What also lay behind their question was the belief, held by many Jews, that when the Messiah did come he would occupy the temple and assume control. Was Jesus then, in acting as he had done, claiming to be the Messiah?

They thought that Jesus would not be able to answer, but he turned the question back on them. Many people believed that John the Baptist had been a prophet from God, so the priests and scribes were afraid to deny that. However, if they had admitted that John was from God, Jesus would no doubt have asked them why they had not accepted him and why they had allowed him to be put to death. So the trick failed.

CHAPTER 12

vv. 1–12   **The rebellious tenants**
At this point, since Jesus is in controversy with the Pharisees, Mark inserts this parable which was obviously aimed at the Pharisees. It is unlike the other parables in Mark, indeed it is unlike most other parables in the gospels, in the sense that the action and reasoning of the tenants is not logical or natural; it could be argued that it is more of an allegory than a parable. In fact some scholars wonder whether it was an authentic parable of Jesus at all.

If it is genuine it appears to be based on the story of the vineyard in Isaiah 5 and concludes with a quotation from Psalm 118: 22. The tenants were the Pharisees, the servants who were sent by the owner were the Old Testament prophets (and possibly the one they killed, v. 5, represented John the Baptist), whilst the son is obviously Jesus. The whole parable predicts the rejection of the Messiah by the Jewish leaders, which leads to the vineyard (the kingdom) being given to others, meaning gentiles. Personally, I regard the parable as a warning to all who believe themselves *owners* of God's gifts, rather than mere trustees. To think of God as an 'absentee landlord' is a very dangerous concept.

vv. 13–17   Paying taxes to Rome

All payment of taxes to Rome was resented by the Jews. Here the Pharisees were probably referring to a particular one levied from A.D. 6 – a poll tax on every Jew.

The trick question, after some sarcastic flattery, was to get Jesus to take sides on the matter. But which side? If he had said, 'Yes, pay, don't argue', they would have told the people that he was supporting something they hated and he would have lost popular support, because the Messiah was expected to free the people from Roman rule. If he had said, 'No, refuse to pay', they would have reported him to the Romans for treason and rebellion. In fact, the Roman representatives (the Herodians) were there as witnesses.

In reply Jesus sent for a silver coin – a denarius. Note that he *sent* for one; part of the trick was to see if he would produce one himself because possession of coins bearing the Roman Emperor's head was illegal in the temple precincts. On one side of the coin was the head of Tiberius, so Jesus said he should be given what was due to him. Tax evasion was not honest; the coin was Caesar's, so it must be given to him. But there was another side to the coin, as there is to life. People are also stamped with the image of God and his kingdom is very different from the Roman kingdom. 'So,' said Jesus, 'give God what belongs to *him*,' i.e. service, time, talent, money and so on.

Greek minted coin of Augustus

Silver denarius of Tiberius   *Coin of Pontius Pilate, minted in Palestine*

vv. 18–27 A bride for seven brothers

The Sadducees' question is based on Deuteronomy 25: 5–10. It was a hypothetical and foolish question. A man was expected to marry his brother's widow, unless there was a son by the marriage, in order to continue the family name. In fact, if he refused, the woman could 'spit in his face'! But *seven* brothers – that was ridiculous!

The Sadducees were priests from wealthy backgrounds, often rich landowners who lived in and around Jerusalem, which may explain why, according to Mark, Jesus had not met them before. Their name may have come from Zadok, a High Priest in the time of David, for Zadok is often written as 'Saddouk' in Greek. They believed in the literal interpretation of the law of Moses and had no patience with the varied interpretations put on those scriptures by the Pharisees and scribes. In fact, they were rather like certain 'exclusive' religious sects today. They did not accept the idea of life after death because there was nothing about it in the written laws. They probably thought it would be easy to put Jesus in his place, but they had a shock.

The trick was probably to try to make Jesus look foolish, or to see whether he agreed with the law of Moses. If he did not, they would have had reason to criticize him.

Jesus's answer, as in the earlier question about marriage in Chapter 10, tells them where they have gone wrong. They are ignorant not only of the scriptures, but, far worse, of the power of God. Life after death is spiritual not physical. The patriarchs – Abraham, Isaac and Jacob – were physically dead but in the spiritual sense were still alive: they were 'alive in God', therefore he is a God of the living.

vv. 28–34 Which commandment is the most important?

A lawyer who had listened carefully to the arguments and was very impressed tried his hand at tripping up Jesus, but he should have known better!

The question is based on the fact that in the Old Testament laws there were 365 'don't's' and 248 'do's'. Which one did Jesus think was the most important? The lawyer was either trying to start an argument with Jesus or testing his knowledge of the Old Testament law. To be more charitable towards him, it may be that he was genuinely wondering whether the mass of religious regulations could profitably be reduced to more manageable proportions and made simpler to understand.

The answer combines Deuteronomy 6: 4–5 with Leviticus 19: 18. If we love God like that, and our neighbour as well, then the rest of the laws will all follow on. If you love a person, you do not want to steal from them, or hurt them or lie to them. In the Good Samaritan Story in Luke 10 Jesus answered another lawyer who asked the question 'Who is my neighbour?' after quoting the same words that Jesus used here.

After this no one dared to ask Jesus any more questions. He went on (v. 38) to give a sharp warning about the influence of some of the scribes.

vv. 41–44 The widow's gift

The arguments had finished and Jesus pointed to a woman who did not waste time arguing about religion – she just put it into practice. In the temple was a big offertory chest with a large trumpet-shaped tube on top, down which people loved to clatter their coins. Sometimes rich men would even hire a trumpeter to call attention to their giving (Matthew 6: 2). The poor widow made no such fuss, she just gave all she had – probably two small coins called 'perutas' about the same size as our present halfpenny. The lesson was this: it is not how much is given but the spirit in which it is given that matters most. She had made a great sacrifice by giving all she had, in sharp contrast to the young rich man (10: 17) who could not go and sell what he had because it would have cost him too much.

CHAPTER 13 SIGNS OF THE END

This strange chapter seems out of place here, indeed some scholars think it is not all attributable to Jesus but is a general composition of Jewish ideas about the end of the age. It is sometimes called the 'Eschatological Discourse' from the Greek word 'eschatos', meaning 'end'. It is the teaching about death, judgement, heaven and hell, and is the type of literature also found in the Old Testament books of Joel and Daniel, as well as in the book of Revelation at the end of the New Testament. The writers predicted future events in vivid terms which, they believed, would lead up to such world-wide wickedness that God would intervene and bring it all to an end. The early Christians, as we can see from some of Paul's letters, lived in expectation of this 'end of the age'.

Some of these predictions did come true, such as the destruction of the temple by the Romans in A.D. 70 after the Jewish rebellion. The disciples *were* persecuted, as we read in the Acts of the Apostles.

The apocalyptic (the word means 'by revelation') 'signs of the end', e.g. wars, famine, earthquakes, seem very foreign to the teaching of Jesus. Remember that earlier he had refused to give such 'signs' (8: 12). Of course events like these have occurred many times in human history – things like families betraying one another (v. 12) happen in times of war and evil government. Much of the 'abomination of desolation' (v. 14) had already been predicted in the Old Testament. In fact the phrase is a quotation from Daniel 11: 31 and 12: 11. The passage about 'signs in the sky' is very similar to Ezekiel 32: 7–8.

This is a difficult chapter to interpret and people hold very different views about it. Some take it literally and look forward (or so it sometimes seems) to the end of the world and the day of judgement, assuming that they are to be among the elect (v. 27). Others look upon it as a description of events which always accompany the breakdown of peace in this world and are the results of human evil. For many centuries people have been expecting 'the end', though without a very clear idea of how it would happen. Personally, I do not think it is part of a Christian's duty to go around preaching a doctrine of damnation and destruction, as though God were just waiting his opportunity to destroy us all. It is true that for the first time in history, as far as we know, the human race now has the means to destroy itself, if not the world, but that assumes that human folly and evil will triumph over goodness and sense, and that God will have to intervene because we have failed to be any better. Is that true Christian belief?

CHAPTER 14

Day 4: Wednesday

Chapters 14 and 15 are sometimes called 'the passion narrative', meaning the story of the suffering and death of Jesus. The New English Bible calls it 'the final conflict'. It was probably the first part of the gospels to be written down and tries to answer three questions:

1. How did Jesus die?
2. Why did he have to die?
3. Who was responsible for his death?

These were most important questions to Mark's early Christian readers.

vv. 1–2   The plotters

The Jewish leaders had clearly decided that Jesus would now have to be put to death. But how? On what charge? How could they do it secretly so as not to cause a riot among Jesus's supporters? Possibly they intended to arrest him and then keep him in custody until the Passover was over. The Passover was an annual festival commemorating the Exodus from Egypt, combined with the springtime festival of 'Maccoth', the feast of unleavened bread (Leviticus 23: 6), and it lasted for seven days.

vv. 3–9   The anointer

Bethany was a small village about 2½ kilometres from Jerusalem, beyond the Mount of Olives.

Whoever the woman was – and there is little evidence to suggest that it was Mary, as John names her in his version of the story (12: 3) – and whoever Simon was, the point is that the woman was evidently trying to pay homage to Jesus; perhaps she was trying to anoint him as the Messiah, but Jesus saw it as an anointment for coming burial. Perhaps that is why the disciples turned on her in such anger, but their anger was hypocritical, as Jesus reminded them, quoting Deuteronomy 15: 11, 'The poor are always there if you really want to help them'.

vv. 10–11   The betrayer

Judas was apparently more angry than any of them (according to John's gospel). All this talk about dying, just because of a foolish woman and her ointment! Judas had had enough of it. He would do something to force Jesus to show himself as the Messiah. Mark devotes only two verses to Judas's treachery and offers no explanation for it. Perhaps we ought to ask ourselves exactly what Judas betrayed. Was it the Messianic secret, the secret meeting-place, the fact that Jesus was apparently prepared to die? Theories abound but evidence is harder to come by. It is disturbing to realize, when reading this, how quickly loyalty can turn to treachery, and often with the excuse that 'the end justifies the means'.

Day 5: Thursday

vv. 12–16 Preparations for the Passover

Was the Last Supper the actual Passover meal? Mark says it was, but John in his gospel says not. The Passover did not begin until sunset on Friday and he therefore maintains that the Last Supper was not the Passover meal (John 13: 1).

So what was the Last Supper? In Mark's account there is no mention of any of the essential ingredients of a Passover meal – the roasted lamb, the bitter herbs, and so on. Some scholars therefore think that this supper was a preparation meal for the Passover – the 'Kiddush', as it was called. It was a meal of friendship customary amongst many Jews in pre-Christian times. On Friday afternoons small groups of friends would meet in private houses for a meal and when the Sabbath began at 6 p.m. the president would take a cup of wine, bless it and pass it round. This was often known as the 'Sanctification of the Sabbath', but if it took place before a great festival (as it often did) it was then used to commemorate that feast, so the Kiddush could have been used to commemorate the Passover. However, a complication here is that the Passover meal had to be eaten in Jerusalem, while the Kiddush could be eaten elsewhere. So why was Jesus so insistent that the meal be eaten in Jerusalem? The important thing, however, is not the meal itself but the meaning of the Last Supper.

Who made all the arrangements for this supper? It must have been Jesus himself or some friends in Jerusalem. A man carrying a water jar would be a most unusual sight, since this was always done by women: it was obviously a pre-arranged secret sign which the two disciples – Luke names them as Peter and John – could see and follow.

Why all this 'cloak-and-dagger' secrecy? Probably because Jesus did not want any interruptions at the Last Supper. It was important that Judas should not have known about it, otherwise he might have betrayed Jesus before the meal started, or at least before it was completed.

Whose house was it? Strong tradition says it was the house of Mary, John Mark's mother, which is mentioned later in Acts 12: 12. If so, John Mark may

A triclinium

well have got some of the information for his gospel from the Christians who met at his house after the death of Jesus.

The table used for the meal was very probably a 'triclinium' – a bench-like table, shaped something like three sides of a square. The 'trestle-table picture' portrayed by many artists is not correct. Only on this triclinium could people recline on their elbows and dip into a central dish (v. 20), using pieces of bread to spoon out morsels of meat. This was one reason why hands had to be very clean!

vv. 17–21 The betrayer is predicted

How did Jesus know what Judas was going to do? He had seen the signs and knew that Judas was the weak link. It seems strange that the other disciples did not make more effort to find out who it was and try to stop him, although what they did was the first step – they asked themselves, searched their own consciences first. They did not shout out heated denials of the charge, instead they looked into their own hearts to see if it could be true.

vv. 22–25 The Last Supper

Does the name imply that there had been previous ones or was it just the last time they could eat together? This was the climax of the ministry of Jesus which everything else had led up to. He would soon be executed. How could he teach the disciples the last and greatest lesson? What would be the best way to impress upon their memories the essence of his life and ministry?

He did a very simple thing: he took the flat, unleavened bread and broke it – 'tore it' would be a better description – and said, 'This is my body'. It was going to be broken and delivered over to ill-treatment and death. Then he poured the wine, glistening red, into a goblet from which they would all drink. 'This is the blood of the covenant,' he said, which meant the 'agreement' with God. The Old Covenant had been made at Mount Sinai, through Moses, and sealed with the Ten Commandments, but this New Covenant, this new approach to God, was to be through the life and death of Jesus.

The idea of a new covenant (some of the more ancient manuscripts of Mark's gospel use the word 'new') is an echo of Jeremiah 31: 31, when he wrote of the need for a new covenant. We also find the idea in Paul's record of the Last Supper in 1 Corinthians 11, which was written about twenty years before Mark's gospel appeared. (The Greek word for 'covenant' is sometimes translated as 'testament' and so the two parts of the Bible became known as the Old Testament and the New Testament as early as the second century A.D.) In Paul's account Jesus says, 'Do this in memory of me', and ever since then the Christian Church has remembered this in its most solemn sacrament, some calling it 'Eucharist', some 'Holy Communion', some 'Mass', some 'the Lord's Supper' and some just 'Sacrament'. It is a worthwhile exercise to find out how it is celebrated in various denominations of the Church.

vv. 27–31   Peter's denial foretold

Jesus quoted from Zechariah 13: 7 about the sheep scattering when the shepherd had been struck down. Peter was the first to deny that he would run away, but Jesus told him that before the cock crowed twice (possibly meaning the Roman trumpet call to mark the watches of the night) he would deny that he had ever known Jesus. Peter, of course, protested his loyalty, as they all did, but words mean little, it is action that counts.

vv. 32–42   Jesus in Gethsemane

The Mount of Olives is a hill just across the Kidron Valley from Jerusalem. Gethsemane – the word means 'oil-press' – was a small garden on the hillside and, according to John's gospel (18: 2), Jesus and the disciples had been there many times. That is how Judas knew where to find him.

The prayers

This passage is sometimes called 'the agony of Jesus'. He was now more alone than he had ever been before, no one could go with him. He asked three of his disciples to keep watch while he prayed. He used a word for God that he had known since childhood – 'Abba', meaning 'Dear Father'. He asked God if there was any other way but the cross. Couldn't this 'cup of suffering' be taken away from him?

It was the third temptation (Luke 4: 9–12) over again. Could the Son of God not be spared the pain and the suffering? But he realized that this could not be and his words, 'Your will be done, not mine', show him practising what he had preached in the Lord's Prayer – 'Thy will be done'.

Three times he prayed and three times the disciples fell asleep on duty. How ironic! They had vowed to *die* for him, but they could not even keep their eyes open for him. It was little wonder they did not know what to say (v. 40).

The Mount of Olives

vv. 43–51 The arrest

The crowd was probably part of the temple police who usually kept order in the temple courts. John says there were also soldiers – presumably Roman troops – but it seems unlikely that the Romans were involved at this point. John also mentions that they carried torches and lanterns, which was most likely as it was pitch dark and they needed some light. That is why Judas kissed Jesus to point out, in the darkness, who was the 'victim'. A kiss was the usual greeting of a teacher by a disciple; it could sometimes be a brushing of both cheeks or it could be a kiss on the hand. It was always a mark of respect and loyalty, which underlines the odiousness of Judas's actions. The sign of friendship had become the signal of treachery.

It is interesting to see how the gospels 'build up' the picture of the arrest. Luke, the doctor, says Jesus healed the man's ear, John names the disciple who used the sword as Peter and the servant as Malchus, but Mark seems rather vague on this point, which is surprising if it is Peter who is the memory behind the gospel.

Some think that the young man who tried to warn Jesus (v. 51) was John Mark himself. This would be a nice thought – roused out of bed when he heard of Judas's intentions, the young man ran to Gethsemane with only his night-shirt on, to try to warn Jesus – but there is not much evidence that it was Mark. Whoever he was he ran away like the rest of the disciples. Neither Luke nor Matthew mentions him.

vv. 53–65 The Jewish trial

It was now very late on Thursday evening or possibly the early hours of Friday. Jesus had two trials (if the first can be called a trial): one before the Jews and the second before the Roman Governor.

The Jewish trial took place before the Sanhedrin Council, although it is improbable that all seventy-one members were present. It was illegal on several counts, some say as many as fourteen, including:

1. It was held at night.
2. The witnesses could not agree, therefore the trial should have been abandoned (Deuteronomy 19: 18–19).
3. Jesus was not given a chance to call any defence witnesses.
4. The High Priest tried to get Jesus to convict himself by admitting to charges which were not true.

The High Priest is named as Caiaphas in Matthew and John. He saw the trial slipping away from the Sanhedrin's power and, in desperation, he tried to get Jesus to incriminate himself by saying whether or not he claimed to be the Messiah, the 'Son of the Blessed One'. Jesus admitted it, and added to it, and the jury had got the evidence they needed – or had they? A *claim* to be the Christ would not amount to blasphemy, at least not in the eyes of a proper Jewish court. But this was not a legal trial and in the haste to get Jesus convicted a false charge was as good as any. If it had been blasphemy then the penalty would have been stoning (Leviticus 24: 16), so why was that penalty not called for? In the Acts of the Apostles (7: 58) it is recorded that Stephen was stoned for the same 'crime'.

The charge that Jesus had said he would 'destroy the temple and in three days build it again' was another example of twisted evidence. He *had* said that (John 2: 19–21), but he had been referring to the resurrection of his body. However, they had got a confession from him so the prisoner now had no rights; Mark gives a vivid account (v. 65) of how the temple police ill-treated Jesus.

vv. 66–72 The disgrace of Peter

This account is so vivid that it can have come only from Peter himself.

How did they know he was a Galilean? Some older translations include the words, in v. 70, 'for your speech betrays you', so he must have had a strong northern accent. Whatever the reason for their suspicion, his reaction was shameful. The man who said he would die for Jesus lost his nerve when confronted by a serving maid. He swore that he had never even set eyes on Jesus. No wonder he broke down and wept.

CHAPTER 15

Day 6: Friday
vv. 1–14 The Roman trial

It was now daybreak on Friday morning. The plan was to get the Romans to pass the death sentence on Jesus – but on what charge? To take Jesus to Pilate (governor of Judaea and Samaria from A.D. 26 to 36) and say that he had claimed to be the Messiah, or Son of God, would not have interested Pilate in the least. He would not have cared if Jesus had claimed to be God himself for he had no belief in the Jewish God and he would have regarded the whole thing as a religious argument for the Jews to settle amongst themselves. So they very cleverly twisted the word 'Messiah' into something of which Pilate would have to take notice: they said that Jesus had claimed to be a 'king' – a political leader, even a revolutionary figure. Hence Pilate's first question was 'Are you the King of the Jews?', to which Jesus replied, 'So you say'. The 'many charges' (v. 3) are not expanded by Mark, but Luke (23: 2) gives the details.

Pilate soon realized that the whole thing was a farce but, according to Mark, did not have the courage to see that justice was done. It is interesting to note how the four gospel writers portray Pilate. In Mark he is weak and indifferent, soon giving way to the demands of the mob; Matthew says he washed his hands of the whole affair; Luke says he tried three times to get Jesus freed and John says he tried six times, giving way only when they threatened to report him to Caesar.

Why was Pilate in such a difficult position when giving judgement? Why did he not insist on justice being done? There are several possible reasons:

1. He was afraid that a riot might start, which would have indicated his inability to keep order.
2. He was afraid that he would be reported to Caesar for sheltering a revolutionary.
3. He gave way to mob violence.
4. He wanted to save his own skin.

The crowd were taking their own revenge on Pilate because they had never forgiven him for marching into Jerusalem with the Roman eagles and the Emperor's image on his banners: the Jews had seen these as 'graven images'.

The Roman standard, showing the imperial eagle

v. 7 Pilate's possible way out

According to Mark, it was the custom for some kind of favour to be shown by the Romans at Passover time, possibly as a sign of 'goodwill'. Although Pilate had never felt less goodwill towards the Jews than he did then, he saw it as a possible way out of his difficulty. He offered to release Jesus as part of this amnesty, but his plan failed: the crowd made his position even worse by demanding that he release Barabbas, a man we know nothing about except that he was a terrorist and convicted murderer – the very last person Pilate would want to let go. But the crowd clamoured for the release of the criminal.

This all sounds as though it could be happening today. The people preferred the man of violence to the man of peace. Perhaps they thought that Barabbas's methods would solve their problems better than the ways of Jesus. Many people think this way today. Why, in so many films and television programmes, is violence portrayed as the only means of persuasion?

vv. 15–20 So, to appease the crowd, Pilate had Jesus flogged, a dreadful punishment usually meted out to condemned slaves and non-Roman citizens (see Deuteronomy 25: 2). The victim was tied to a stone pillar and lashed with whips. Many prisoners died under this ordeal, making crucifixion unnecessary, so Jesus must have been physically very strong to have withstood this punishment. After the flogging he was handed over to be crucified and, again, as a condemned man no longer had any rights. The soldiers could treat him as they wished. Notice the cruel mockery of that word 'king' – the purple robe, the 'crown' of thorns (which was a grim joke based on the wreath given to victorious athletes), the 'Hail, King of the Jews' (v. 18), which was a version of their own 'Hail, Caesar'. Mark says this cruelty was carried out by the whole battalion, which would be several hundred men.

v. 21 When they had tired of it all they took him to the hill of execution outside the city walls. The name 'Golgotha' was from the Aramaic for 'skull', and from the Latin word 'calvaria', which means the same thing, we get the name 'Calvary'. The hill was either shaped like a skull or got its name from the fact that it was the place of death.

The person to be crucified had to carry the cross-beam (not the whole cross – that would have been far too heavy) tied across his back. After all he had been through, it was no wonder that Jesus collapsed. He had had no food, no sleep, no medical attention, and he had suffered a terrible beating and brutality. Simon from Cyrene in North Africa was probably a Jew visiting Jerusalem on business or possibly for the Passover festival. One moment he was a spectator along the road – sometimes called the 'Via Dolorosa' (the way of sorrows) – and the next he was forced to carry the cross-beam which the soldiers had to take away from Jesus. One wonders what was said as the two men stumbled along together. Simon's two sons were obviously well known to Mark's readers as he mentions only their first names (v. 21), so it seems that they became Christians. Perhaps it was because of what their father had told them about the remarkable man who had gone to his death without one word of resentment against his enemies.

vv. 22–27   The crucifixion
Mark does not dwell on the details; there are no 'close-ups' of the victim's face and his agony. Good writers do not need to spell out the sordidness of such terrible events, they leave it to the imagination. It is a saddening thought that curiosity can become ghoulish and horror an entertainment.

Crucifixion was one of the cruellest forms of death ever devised. When the victim reached the place of execution his arms were tied, or his hands nailed, to the ends of the cross-beam. This beam was then raised and fastened to a permanent upright post and the victim's feet nailed to the lower part of the post. He was then left to die – from exposure, thirst and slow suffocation as the body sagged. Sometimes this could take days.

Someone offered Jesus some drugged wine to take away the pain but, according to Mark (v. 23), he refused it. The soldiers who had carried out the crucifixion were entitled to whatever the prisoner possessed, so they gambled for Jesus's clothes at the foot of the cross, thus fulfilling the prophecy in Psalm 22: 18.

v. 25   *The time*   It was nine o'clock in the morning when Jesus was crucified, with two criminals as companions and a notice of his 'crime' nailed to the top of the cross. According to Mark it read 'The King of the Jews'. In John's gospel (19: 19) the full inscription on the cross is given – 'Jesus of Nazareth the King of the Jews'. The letters I.N.R.I., which are the abbreviation of the Latin 'Iesus Nazarenus Rex Iudaeorum', can often be seen in churches and on crosses today. The irony is that Jesus had never claimed to be a king in that sense; in fact, he had always fought against any temptation to be so.

vv. 29–32   The mocking of Jesus by the passers-by and the priests is a reminder of Psalm 22: 7 and Psalm 109: 25. They wanted to see some dramatic miraculous escape from the cross, then they would have believed that he was the Messiah. They could not understand any sign of Messiahship other than the selfish one of the Messiah saving himself. They failed to see that sacrifice and suffering could be a form of success.

vv. 33–39   The death of Jesus
At noon there was a strange darkness which lasted for three hours. Luke (23: 45) says it was some kind of eclipse, but it is more likely to have been a heavy storm or low clouds. It is important because of the Old Testament belief that darkness was the time of judgement. Jesus's cry of anguish and loneliness, which Mark gives in the original Aramaic (v. 34), is often seen as a cry of despair, but Psalm 22, of which this sentence is the first line, contains other

verses of great hope and faith. The fact that the onlookers thought he was calling Elijah shows how they misunderstood his words.

The curtain of the temple, which was torn down as Jesus died (v. 38), was the division between the most sacred part of the temple and the rest of the building, i.e. between the place where only the High Priest could go and the place where ordinary worshippers could stand. It represented the removal of the barrier which had been erected between God and man: this is what the death of Jesus symbolizes.

The centurion's verdict (v. 39) referred to the way in which Jesus died. He had seen many men die by crucifixion – some cursing, some pleading, some fearful – but never had he seen a man face death like this, with forgiveness on his lips. It reminds us that the important thing is not when or where death comes, but how one faces up to it.

vv. 40–41   The women who watched

It is sometimes pointed out that it was the women who stayed and the men who ran away from Golgotha.

Mary Magdalene (so called because she came from the village of Magdala) was the one, according to Luke 8: 2, from whom Jesus had cast out 'seven devils', which may well have meant some kind of mental illness rather than that she was an immoral woman, as some seem to think.

According to Matthew 27: 56, Salome was the mother of the sons of Zebedee, i.e. James and John.

vv. 42–47   The burial

By this time it was about five o'clock and the Sabbath would shortly begin (at sunset). According to the Old Testament law (Deuteronomy 22: 23) it was an offence to leave a body hanging overnight, so it had to be buried. We do not know much about Joseph of Arimathaea (Arimathaea was a village near the town of Lydda to the north-west of Jerusalem) except that he must have been a very brave as well as a very good man. To ask for the body of a convicted man was to risk being associated with the criminal. Also, if he was a member of the Sanhedrin as Mark says, he would have to face their anger too. Being a rich man, Joseph had a private family tomb – a cave cut out of the rock with ledges along the sides. So Jesus, believed to have been born in a cave, was buried in one.

The linen sheet or shroud (v. 46) has frequently been the subject of much controversy. A piece of linen cloth, about 4 metres long, has been kept in a special shrine in the cathedral at Turin since 1578 and many people believe it is the sheet in which Joseph wrapped the body of Jesus, though scientific tests are still being carried out on it. According to John's gospel, Joseph also brought ointment and precious spices with which to anoint the body, as was the Jewish custom. Then, since the hour was late and the Sabbath about to begin, he put Jesus's body into the tomb and rolled a large round stone across the entrance to prevent any interference with the body and to stop anyone stealing the valuable spices. Matthew tells us that the stone was also sealed and guards posted outside (27: 66).

The tomb of Herod in Jerusalem, with a round stone to close the entrance

Why is this day called 'Good Friday'? Although dreadful things happened, to Christians it was a day of triumph. Of course, to the disciples and followers at the time it was a day of defeat, and to the enemies of Jesus it was a day of victory or at least of 'justice' being achieved. However, to Christians looking back on its significance it was the supreme example of the love of God through Christ and the day on which evil, in all its forms, did its worst but could not defeat the goodness of God.

Day 7: the Sabbath

No work was allowed on this day so nothing could be done to embalm the body or to visit the tomb.

CHAPTER 16

vv. 1–8   Day 8: Sunday
The resurrection

We now call this Sunday Easter Day from the old Anglo-Saxon name Eostre, a goddess whose festival was celebrated in the spring, but it is in fact the resurrection of Jesus that is commemorated. The burial had been a hurried affair: there were no mourners, no weeping, no time to embalm the body. The women had had to wait until the Sabbath was over (on the Saturday evening) before they could buy spices and then it was too late to carry out the embalming, so they had to wait until the Sunday morning. At first light they were there, but the body had gone. The tomb was empty except for a young man (probably an angel) who told the women not to be afraid, though naturally they were. He told them to go and tell the disciples – especially Peter since he needed a special word of forgiveness for his denial of Jesus – that Jesus would meet them in Galilee, but the women just fled and said nothing to anyone.

And that, v. 8, is where Mark's gospel, according to the most reliable ancient manuscripts, abruptly ends. He ends in the middle of a sentence; the actual translation is, 'for they were afraid of . . . .'

Why did Mark end so suddenly?
There are several possibilities though the real reason may never be known.

1. The original ending was lost or torn off.
2. Mark was arrested as he wrote or even killed.
3. The real ending has been included in another gospel.

Whatever the explanation, it is evident that vv. 9–20 are the work of someone else, for they are not written in Mark's style. In fact the passages in other gospels and in the Acts of the Apostles on which vv. 9–20 are based can easily be identified: for example, v. 12 refers to the walk to Emmaus, Luke 24: 13–35; v. 15 refers to Matthew 28: 19; and v. 19 refers to Acts 1: 9. Some scholars maintain that vv. 9–20 were the work of a second-century presbyter named Ariston.

Does this really matter, however? In a sense, the gospel is always unfinished. It is a continuous story, never completed, an unfinished task to be carried on by all generations; it must never be regarded as ended or completed. The unwritten pages are the lives of Christian people throughout the ages. In that sense the story is a living one and each individual adds their own ending to it.

Postscript

At the beginning we said that if we possessed only one gospel instead of four, our understanding of the life and teaching of Jesus would be restricted, and it has been obvious that in Mark's account much familiar material is missing. We noticed the absence of any birth stories, details of the temptations, the Lord's Prayer, the Sermon on the Mount, and so on. All these, of course, are seen in other gospels, together with details about John the Baptist, more of the parables, and resurrection appearances. However, it is interesting to look at the gospels separately and to see how Luke and Matthew use and expand (and sometimes change) Mark's account. This puts the synoptic idea clearly into focus, whereas a general 'Life of Christ', combining all the gospels, can cause confusion for the student. It has always been my contention that to 'tease out' the strands of the story initially and then combine them eventually is much more rewarding than retarding. Therefore, having seen how Mark gives the broad outline of Jesus's life, we can go on to see how the other writers fit in finer details.

Appendix

Incident	Mark	Luke	Matthew
John the Baptist	1: 1–8	3: 3–17	3: 1–12
The baptism of Jesus	1: 9–11	3: 21–22	3: 13–17
The temptations	1: 12–13	4: 1–13	4: 1–11
Call of the disciples	1: 16–20	5: 1–11	4: 18–22
A day in the life of Jesus	1: 21–39	4: 31–44	8: 14–15 (part)
Healing the leper	1: 40–45	5: 12–16	8: 2–4
Man lowered through the roof	2: 1–12	5: 17–26	9: 1–8
The call of Levi	2: 13–14	5: 27–28	9: 9
Eating with tax-collectors	2: 15–17	5: 29–32	9: 10–13
The question of fasting	2: 18–20	5: 33–39	9: 14–17
The cornfield	2: 23–28	6: 1–5	12: 1–8
The man with the crippled arm	3: 1–6	6: 6–11	12: 9–14
The twelve disciples	3: 13–19	6: 12–16	10: 1–4
'He is mad,' said the scribes	3: 22–30	11: 15–23	12: 24–32
Jesus's family	3: 31–35	8: 19–21	12: 46–50
The sower and the soil	4: 3–9	8: 4–8	13: 1–9
The purpose of parables	4: 10–12	8: 9–10	13: 10–15
Explanation of the sower	4: 13–20	8: 11–15	13: 18–23
The lamp	4: 21–23	11: 33	5: 15
The measure	4: 24–25	6: 38	7: 2
The mystery of growth	4: 26–29		
The mustard seed	4: 30–34	13: 18–19	13: 31–32
Calming the storm	4: 35–41	8: 22–25	8: 23–27
Legion, the lunatic	5: 1–20	8: 26–39	8: 28–34
The daughter of Jairus, the woman with haemorrhages	5: 21–43	8: 40–56	9: 18–26
In the synagogue at Nazareth	6: 1–6	(4: 16–30?)	13: 53–58
The mission of the Twelve	6: 7–13	9: 1–6	10: 5–14
Herod and Jesus	6: 14–16	9: 7–9	14: 1–2
The death of John the Baptist	6: 17–29	3: 19–20	14: 3–12
Feeding the five thousand	6: 30–44 (also in John 6: 1–13)	9: 10–17	14: 13–21
Walking on the water	6: 45–52 (also in John 6: 16–21)		14: 22–23
Things that defile a person	7: 1–23		15: 1–20
The foreign woman's daughter	7: 24–30		15: 21–28
Healing of the deaf man	7: 31–37		
Feeding the four thousand	8: 1–10		15: 32–39
The influence of the Pharisees	8: 14–21		16: 5–12
The blind man at Bethsaida	8: 22–26		

Incident	Mark	Luke	Matthew
Peter's confession	8: 27–33	9: 18–21	16: 13–20
First prophecy of death	8: 34–38	9: 22	16: 21–23
The transfiguration	9: 2–8	9: 28–36	17: 1–8
Questions about Elijah	9: 9–13		17: 9–13
The epileptic boy	9: 14–29	9: 37–42	17: 14–21
Second prediction of death	9: 30–32	9: 43–45	17: 22–23
The question of greatness	9: 33–37	9: 46–48	18: 1–5
'He who is not against us'	9: 38–40	9: 49–50	
Leading little ones astray	9: 42–50	17: 1–2 (part)	18: 6–10
Marriage and divorce	10: 1–12	16: 18 (part)	19: 1–9
Welcoming the children	10: 13–16	18: 15–17	19: 13–15
The rich young man	10: 17–22	18: 18–23	19: 16–22
The danger of riches	10: 23–27	18: 24–27	19: 23–26
The rewards you can expect!	10: 28–31	18: 28–30	19: 27–30
Third prediction of death	10: 32–34	18: 31–33	19: 27–30
James's and John's request	10: 35–45		20: 20–28
A blind man at Jericho	10: 46–52	18: 35–43	20: 29–34 (two men)
Entry into Jerusalem	11: 1–11 (also in John 12: 12–16)	19: 28–38	21: 1–9
The fig tree and its meaning	11: 12–14, 20–25		21: 18–22
Cleansing the temple	11: 15–19 (also in John 2: 12–22)	19: 45–48	21: 12–17
By whose authority?	11: 27–33	20: 1–8	21: 23–27
Parable of the vineyard	12: 1–12	20: 9–19	21: 33–46
Taxes to Caesar	12: 13–17	20: 20–26	22: 15–22
Question on resurrection	12: 18–27	20: 27–40	22: 23–33
The greatest commandment	12: 28–34	(10: 25–28 similar)	22: 34–40
The Messiah and David	12: 35–40	20: 41–44	22: 41–46
The widow's gift	12: 41–44	21: 1–4	
Troubles and tribulations	13	21 (part)	24 (part)
The plot to kill Jesus	14: 1–2	22: 1–2	26: 1–5
The anointing at Bethany	14: 3–9 (similar story in John 12: 1–8)	(7: 36–50 similar)	26: 6–13
Judas goes to betray Jesus	14: 10–11	22: 3–6	26: 14–16
Preparations for the Last Supper	14: 12–16	22: 7–13	26: 17–19
The Last Supper	14: 17–25 (also 1 Corinthians 11: 23–26)	22: 14–30	26: 20–29
Peter's denial foretold	14: 26–31	22: 31–34	26: 30–35
In Gethsemane	14: 32–42	22: 40–45	26: 36–46
The arrest	14: 43–50	22: 47–53	26: 47–56
The young man who ran away	14: 51–52		
Jesus and the Sanhedrin	14: 53–65	22: 54, 63–71	26: 57–68

Incident	Mark	Luke	Matthew
Peter denies Jesus	14: 66–72	22: 55–62	26: 69–75
Jesus before Pilate	15: 1–15	23: 1–5, 13–25	27: 1–2, 11–26
Mocking by the soldiers	15: 16–20		27: 27–31
The crucifixion	15: 21–32	23: 26–43	27: 32–44
The death of Jesus	15: 33–39	23: 44–48	27: 45–54
The burial	15: 40–47	23: 49–56	27: 55–61
The resurrection: the women visit the tomb	16: 1–8	24: 1–11	28: 1–8
Various appearances of Jesus	16: 9–20 (not in original manuscripts)	24: 13–49	28: 9–10, 16–20